JOHN O'HARA

LITERATURE AND LIFE SERIES
(Formerly Modern Literature and World Dramatists)
GENERAL EDITOR: PHILIP WINSOR

Selected list of titles:

SHERWOOD ANDERSON   *Welford Dunaway Taylor*
JAMES BALDWIN   *Carolyn Wedin Sylvander*
SAUL BELLOW   *Brigitte Scheer-Schäzler*
ANTHONY BURGESS   *Samuel Coale*
TRUMAN CAPOTE   *Helen S. Garson*
WILLA CATHER   *Dorothy Tuck McFarland*
JOHN CHEEVER   *Samuel Coale*
JOSEPH CONRAD   *Martin Tucker*
JOAN DIDION   *Katherine Usher Henderson*
JOHN DOS PASSOS   *George J. Becker*
THEODORE DREISER   *James Lundquist*
T. S. ELIOT   *Burton Raffel*
WILLIAM FAULKNER   *Joachim Seyppel*
F. SCOTT FITZGERALD   *Rose Adrienne Gallo*
FORD MADOX FORD   *Sondra J. Stang*
E. M. FORSTER   *Claude J. Summers*
JOHN FOWLES   *Barry N. Olshen*
ROBERT FROST   *Elaine Barry*
ELLEN GLASGOW   *Marcelle Thiébaux*
ROBERT GRAVES   *Katherine Snipes*
ERNEST HEMINGWAY   *Samuel Shaw*
JOHN IRVING   *Gabriel Miller*
CHRISTOPHER ISHERWOOD   *Claude J. Summers*
SARAH ORNE JEWETT   *Josephine Donovan*
JAMES JOYCE   *Armin Arnold*
KEN KESEY   *Barry H. Leeds*
RING LARDNER   *Elizabeth Evans*
D. H. LAWRENCE   *George J. Becker*
C. S. LEWIS   *Margaret Patterson Hannay*
SINCLAIR LEWIS   *James Lundquist*
ROBERT LOWELL   *Burton Raffel*
NORMAN MAILER   *Philip H. Bufithis*
BERNARD MALAMUD   *Sheldon J. Hershinow*
MARY MCCARTHY   *Willene Schaefer Hardy*
CARSON MCCULLERS   *Richard M. Cook*
JAMES A. MICHENER   *George J. Becker*
MARIANNE MOORE   *Elizabeth Phillips*

(*continued on last page of book*)

JOHN O'HARA

Robert Emmet Long

FREDERICK UNGAR PUBLISHING CO.
NEW YORK

Copyright © 1983 by Frederick Ungar Publishing Co., Inc.
Printed in the United States of America

Library of Congress Cataloging in Publication Data

Long, Robert Emmet.
  John O'Hara.

  (Literature and life series)
  Bibliography: p. 185.
  Includes index.
  1. O'Hara, John. 2. Novelists, American—20th
century—Biography. I. Title. II. Series.
PS3529.H29Z75 1983   813'.52 [B]   83-12387
ISBN 0-8044-2541-8

*For Robert E. Long, My Father,
in Memory*

Contents

Chronology

<table>
<tr><td>1905</td><td>John Henry O'Hara born January 31, Pottsville, Pennsylvania, first of eight children of Dr. Patrick H. and Katharine Delaney O'Hara</td></tr>
<tr><td>1919</td><td>Drives his father's car during the influenza epidemic, the remembered experiences of "The Doctor's Son"</td></tr>
<tr><td>1920-21</td><td>Attends Fordham Preparatory School, Bronx; dismissed</td></tr>
<tr><td>1921-22</td><td>Attends Keystone State Normal School, Kutztown, Pa.; dismissed</td></tr>
<tr><td>1922-23</td><td>Works at various manual jobs</td></tr>
<tr><td>1923-24</td><td>Attends Niagara Preparatory School, Niagara Falls, N.Y.; chosen valedictorian but because of drinking incident is not allowed to graduate</td></tr>
<tr><td>1924</td><td>Begins work as reporter on Pottsville Journal</td></tr>
<tr><td>1925</td><td>Dr. O'Hara dies, leaving family in straitened circumstances</td></tr>
<tr><td>1927</td><td>Resolves to leave Pottsville; works way to Europe as waiter on ocean liner; hitchhikes to Chicago in unsuccessful attempt to find newspaper work</td></tr>
<tr><td>1928</td><td>Leaves Pottsville for New York City; works briefly for New York Herald Tribune; sells first piece to The New Yorker. Meets Dorothy Parker, Robert Benchley, and Wolcott Gibbs</td></tr>
<tr><td>1929</td><td>Has variety of short-term jobs—for Time, Editor and Publisher, New York Daily Mirror; becomes frequent contributor to The New Yorker</td></tr>
</table>

1930   Movie critic and radio columnist for New York *Morning Telegraph,* and works for Heywood Broun

1931   Marries Helen Petit, a young Wellesley-educated actress. Honeymoon in Bermuda. Has variety of jobs—as reporter for *The New Yorker* and publicist for Warner Brothers and Benjamin Sonnenberg public relations

1932   Works for New York publicity department of RKO. Frequents speakeasies; Wolcott Gibbs, Dorothy Parker, James Thurber, and others claim O'Hara has "special" talent

1933   Turbulent marriage ends as Helen Petit O'Hara obtains divorce in Reno; works briefly as managing editor for Pittsburgh newspaper, and experiences near-suicidal despair; returns to New York and begins *Appointment in Samarra.* Friendship with F. Scott Fitzgerald, who reads draft of O'Hara's novel

1934   Editor of ship's newspaper during Caribbean cruise of *Kungsholm;* achieves instant success and critical acclaim with publication of *Appointment in Samarra;* script-writing assignment with Paramount Pictures

1935   Visits Italy and France. Publishes *The Doctor's Son* and *Butterfield 8*

1937   Marries Belle Mulford Wylie of New York City and Quogue, Long Island; begins his lifelong connection with Quogue as summer resident

1938   Publishes *Hope of Heaven; Pal Joey* stories appear in *The New Yorker*

1939   Further film writing in Hollywood; publishes *Files on Parade,* and is called "master" of the short story

1940   Writes column for *Newsweek,* covering theatre and movies; continues column until 1942. *Pal Joey* stories appear as book and as musical play with script by O'Hara, music by Richard Rodgers, and lyrics by Lorenz Hart

1941-43   Attempts to join armed forces; does work for Office of Inter-American Affairs; OSS training. Works on unproduced plays

1944   Correspondent for *Liberty*, summer 1944, attached to Task Force 38 in Pacific, aboard *Intrepid*

1945   Birth of daughter, Wylie Delaney O'Hara; publication of story collection *Pipe Night*

1946   Hollywood. Works on *Cass Timberlane* screenplay. Publishes *Here's O'Hara*, containing three novels and twenty stories

1947   Publishes *Hellbox*, story collection

1949   Moves to Princeton. Publishes *A Rage to Live*, his first Pennsylvania novel since *Appointment in Samarra*

1951   Publishes *The Farmers Hotel*, set in Pennsylvania

1952   Revival of *Pal Joey* on New York stage receives the Drama Critics' Award

1953   Near death following hemorrhage of gastric ulcer; gives up drinking permanently

1954   Belle Wylie O'Hara dies from congenital heart weakness

1955   Marries Katharine ("Sister") Barnes Bryan, whose marriage to Joseph Bryan III has ended in divorce; *Ten North Frederick*, novel about Pottsville (the fictional Gibbsville), is published and receives the National Book Award

1956   Hollywood script writing; publishes *A Family Party*

1957   National Institute of Arts and Letters confers a membership on O'Hara; moves to "Linebrook," the O'Haras' new house in countryside near Princeton; O'Hara's closing period of remarkable productivity begins

1958   Publishes *From the Terrace*, his longest novel, recording the first half of the twentieth century in North America

1960   Publishes *Ourselves to Know* and *Sermons and Soda-Water*

1961   Publishes *Assembly* (stories) and *Five Plays*

1963   Publishes *Elizabeth Appleton* and *The Hat on the Bed* (stories)

1964   Receives the Award of Merit in Fiction for the Novel from the American Academy of Arts and Letters; publishes *The Horse Knows the Way* (stories)

1965   Publishes *The Lockwood Concern;* has sixtieth birthday

1966   Publishes *Waiting for Winter* (stories)

1967   Publishes *The Instrument*

1968   Publishes *And Other Stories*

1969   Publishes *Lovey Childs*

1970   Finishes *The Ewings* in February, and begins *The Second Ewings* four days later. Dies in sleep, April 11, at "Linebrook," home outside Princeton

1

John O'Hara:
The Contour of a Life

John O'Hara was a force in American fiction for more than thirty-five years, from the middle of the Depression until his death in 1970. In his earlier years he was best known as a writer of short stories, many of which appeared in *The New Yorker*, but he was later recognized as a novelist who published prolifically and whose imagination seemed inexhaustibly furnished with fictional situations. He became one of the most celebrated American writers of his time, and like Faulkner and Wolfe he created a fictional "region"—the hard-coal mining country of northeastern Pennsylvania. It was in this area that he was born on January 31, 1905, the first of eight children of Dr. Patrick H. and Katharine Delaney O'Hara. Pottsville, the town of his birth, a community of twenty-five thousand population and the county seat, contained a mixture of the upper and middle classes, the poor, and the desperately poor, and it was ethnically diverse. The O'Haras were distinctly Irish, and the Irish were a factor in the town, important and influential but not ranking at the very top of the social pyramid. Dr. Patrick O'Hara had a successful medical practice, and lived on the town's best street—Mahantongo Street, the "Lantenengo Street" of O'Hara's fiction.

John O'Hara's mother was a gifted mimic and storyteller, as O'Hara was to be himself, and he possessed in adult years perhaps the most acute and finely tuned mimetic gift in modern American fiction. But it was Dr. O'Hara who affected his son most directly. A strong-willed, hard-working, disciplined professional man, he was also fiercely independent and had an explosive temper. He gave his son a number of early advantages, but passed on to him, too, an intractable disposition and ungovernable temper. O'Hara later remarked that the distance that always separated his father and himself was caused by their being so much alike. Neither could bend sufficiently to create a middle ground of understanding, and the result was shattering for the boy, who keenly felt his father's withholding of love and approval.

Dr. O'Hara had some reason to be displeased with his son as he was growing up. He did poorly in school and was a discipline problem. For three terms, beginning in February 1920, he attended the Fordham Preparatory School, which was attached to Fordham University and supervised by the Jesuits. O'Hara's grades were so poor that the Jesuits advised his father to try placing him elsewhere; but in the next school, after two terms, the headmaster offered the same advice. For a year, Dr. O'Hara put his son to work as a laborer in the coal-mining region, and then tried another school, the Niagara Preparatory School, attached to his own alma mater, Niagara University. This time O'Hara distinguished himself, being named valedictorian, and Dr. O'Hara came personally to attend the graduation exercises—only to be confronted by his son's disgrace. On the night before graduation, O'Hara had gone to a speakeasy, appeared on campus the following morning in a tipsy state, was reported by a proctor, stripped of his valedictory honors, and dismissed from the school.

Dr. O'Hara had considered sending his son to Yale, but at this point he put him to work, instead, for a probationary period of a year. Although he regarded his son's interest in becoming a writer with incomprehension, Dr. O'Hara used his influence to have him hired as a cub reporter on the Pottsville *Journal*. John lived at home with his family, and from time to time sparks flew between father and son. Dr. O'Hara, who was strictly abstemious, objected strongly to his son's use of alcohol, and at one point warned him: "Keep up this way and you'll be dead before you're thirty." O'Hara is supposed to have retorted that by then he would be in *Who's Who*, and, as it turned out, he was.

Within a year Dr. O'Hara fell ill with Bright's disease; his health failed rapidly, and he died in March 1925, at the age of fifty-eight, when John O'Hara was twenty. Dr. O'Hara's funeral, an immense affair, with more than twenty Catholic priests present and over forty cars in the cortege, was an indication of the regard in which he was held in the town. But, unfortunately, he had been careless in the management of his financial affairs, and the family went suddenly from prosperity to genteel poverty. O'Hara, to whom his father's last words had been "Poor John," began to drink heavily, and was eventually fired from his job at the Pottsville *Journal*. During the same period he also fell in love with Margaretta Archbold, daughter of one of the town's wealthiest white Anglo-Saxon Protestant families. The Archbold family sent their daughter to a distant boarding school to discourage the relationship, objecting to O'Hara as a young man who drank and had an unruly temper. O'Hara's reputation in the community deteriorated rapidly, and he was only too anxious to leave the town that he would later write about compulsively.

During the summer of 1927, O'Hara worked his way to Europe as a waiter aboard an ocean liner, and on his return hitchhiked to Chicago, where he lived in a series of flophouses while he made an unsuccessful search for newspaper work. He returned to Pottsville, but in February 1928 left for New York, where he was hired as a reporter for the New York *Herald Tribune*. Six months later he was dismissed for absenteeism due to drinking. A period followed of many short-term jobs with newspapers from which he either quit or was fired. Newspaper work interested him much less than the fiction he was writing and had begun to publish in *The New Yorker*—chiefly sketches and vignettes for its "Talk of the Town" column. O'Hara became a habitué of New York speakeasies, and of one in particular, Tony Soma's on West Fifty-second Street, where he knew Robert Benchley, James Thurber, Heywood Broun, and other writers. His closest friends were Dorothy Parker and Wolcott Gibbs, for whom his fictional Gibbsville, based on Pottsville, was named. It was said of O'Hara at this time that he looked as if he had bought his clothes at rummage sales in the vicinity of a university, and there were times, indeed, when he was so poor that he went for days without eating. But among the circle at Tony Soma's, and particularly to Dorothy Parker, one of his earliest and strongest admirers, O'Hara had already been recognized as a young writer of distinct promise.

In 1929, O'Hara met Helen Petit, then twenty-two and a graduate of Wellesley. She had, in addition, a master's degree from Columbia, had studied at the Sorbonne, and had played the part of the ingénue opposite Eddie Albert in *Room Service* on Broadway. Helen Petit was the only child of a woman whose husband had left her, and who lived comfortably in Brooklyn with a wealthy bachelor brother. O'Hara married Helen Petit in February 1931, but partly because of his unsteady employment and his mother-in-law's ceaseless interference in their marriage, the relationship was stormy. It became stormier still when O'Hara began to harbor suspicions, apparently groundless, of his wife's interest in other men. When he was drinking heavily he sometimes abused her verbally in public places. He is supposed once to have thrown her out of a moving cab. In 1933, Helen Petit obtained a divorce from O'Hara in Reno on grounds of "extreme cruelty." O'Hara became despondent and was at times on the verge of suicide.

Yet at this low point in his life, while living in an inexpensive hotel room in New York, O'Hara wrote his first novel, *Appointment in Samarra,* and it made him famous. Paramount studios, after reading the novel in galleys, hired O'Hara to write dialogue for films, and he began his career as a sometime Hollywood writer, like James Malloy, who appears in two of his novels and more than a dozen stories. In Hollywood, O'Hara frequented such nightspots as the Trocadero and the Coconut Grove, and he became part of the circle at Robert Benchley's Garden of Allah bungalow. On almost any afternoon, Benchley's living room would be crowded with celebrities—with such actors and writers as Cedric Hardwicke, Herbert Marshall, Humphrey Bogart, Clifford Odets, John Steinbeck, Dorothy Parker, and F. Scott Fitzgerald.

O'Hara had begun corresponding with Fitzgerald several years earlier, and he remained for O'Hara a kind of idol.[1] Asked to give the most important literary influences on his career, he named Fitzgerald first, and he often commented or reflected on Fitzgerald in his letters. For many years he was in the habit of drawing parallels between Fitzgerald's career and his own, until he finally concluded that the resemblances had existed chiefly in his own mind—they were the product of a deep and lifelong fascination with the slightly older writer. Both had come from Irish Catholic backgrounds, were fascinated by the rich, and had "created" their age, including the destructive forces just beneath the surfaces of American life that blighted their characters' aspirations. Both had a peculiarly Irish pessimism about life, Fitzgerald's expressed more romantically, O'Hara's naturalistically. But perhaps the ultimate source of O'Hara's sense of kinship with Fitzgerald was that the latter was enormously talented, a high achiever in fiction, as O'Hara aspired to be.

As a personality in Hollywood, O'Hara was frequently moody, sometimes bellicose, at other times shy and withdrawn, solitary and brooding. The writer William Saroyan, a Hollywood friend of O'Hara's, described him as "one of the loneliest souls" he had ever seen.[2] The youthful, melancholic O'Hara eventually entered into fiction as the model for Hector Connolly in Nancy Hale's novel *The Prodigal Woman* (1942)—a heavy-drinking, violent Irish writer tormented by his lost Catholicism and his divorce. Certainly O'Hara had difficulty in his relationships with women, who were at first attracted to him but then, noting his drinking and outbursts, drew back. One of his biographers describes him, after drinking late at night, turning up at the doors of women who had spurned him.

Fortunately for O'Hara, one woman, Belle Mulford Wylie, did not. Belle Wylie had developed a crush on O'Hara, the famous author of *Appointment in Samarra,* even before meeting him in Hollywood in 1936. The attraction was reciprocated, and during their engagement, O'Hara followed Belle to Quogue, Long Island, a community of low-keyed affluence where the Wylies had a summer home, and he courted not only her but also her family, presenting himself to them as a model citizen and future son-in-law. In December 1937, when he was thirty-two and she twenty-four, O'Hara and Belle were married. He was by then a recognized younger writer, the author of two novels— *Appointment in Samarra* and *Butterfield 8*—and a highly praised collection of short stories, *The Doctor's Son.*

In 1938 O'Hara published his third novel, *Hope of Heaven*, set in Hollywood, but most of his work of that time was in the short story. In the period of the late 1930s he contributed 134 stories to *The New Yorker* alone. One of these *New Yorker* pieces, "Pal Joey," published in 1938, led to O'Hara's writing a series of tales dealing with the same antihero, a sleazy nightclub singer and "heel." *Pal Joey* was published as a book in 1940, and in the same year O'Hara adapted the work for the stage, in collaboration with Richard Rodgers and Lorenz Hart. In December 1940, *Pal Joey* opened on Broadway to critical acclaim. Its unconventional hero and subtly modulated, sophisticated cynicism made it one of the most innovative and influential of modern American musical plays. The commercial success of *Pal Joey*, which enjoyed a lengthy run, made O'Hara affluent for the first time in his life.

O'Hara's marriage to Belle Wylie also proved to be fortunate. According to O'Hara's biographers, her devotion to her husband was legendary among her friends. She accommodated herself to his nocturnal work habits, helped in every way she could, and accepted his heavy drinking without complaint. O'Hara remained a prickly and difficult man; but his life was now more under control than it had been previously. In the late 1930s, the O'Haras lived in Hollywood for a time, where O'Hara did more work for films, and in New York, where they leased a Manhattan apartment with a lofty view of the East River. A number of stories and anecdotes about O'Hara, some having to do with his mourned-over lack of a college education, belong to this time. Ernest Hemingway, a drinking companion of O'Hara's when he came to New York, once received an unexpected royalty check and suggested to friends that it be used to send O'Hara to Yale.

In 1941, when the United States entered World War II, O'Hara, then thirty-six, attempted to enlist first in the army and then in the Marine Corps, but was turned down for a variety of medical reasons—he had a chronic ulcer and high blood pressure. Through the influence of his friend James Forrestal, then under secretary of the navy, O'Hara was accepted into the OSS, but within a month was sent home with pneumonia, after having failed to pass the medical examination. In 1944, he served briefly as a correspondent for *Liberty* magazine, attached to the aircraft carrier *Intrepid* in the Pacific, an assignment so marginal that O'Hara felt humiliated. O'Hara's only child, a daughter, Wylie Delaney O'Hara, was born in 1945, brightening a period of frustration and discouragement. In 1949 O'Hara came to attention again as a novelist with his large, sprawling family chronicle *A Rage to Live*, set in "the Region." *A Rage to Live* became a huge commercial success, but was savaged by reviewers. One review in particular, by Brendan Gill in *The New Yorker*, was especially embittering to O'Hara. More than any other single individual, O'Hara had "created" the *New Yorker* short story and been its most frequent contributor in fiction. He not only felt betrayed by the sharply hostile review but even became convinced of a conspiracy among *New Yorker* colleagues to denigrate him, and he refused to contribute further to the magazine. In 1949, he left New York to live in Princeton.

In 1952, O'Hara returned to prominence when *Pal Joey* was revived for the stage and enjoyed a record run. During the following year, however, O'Hara suffered a breakdown in his health. He collapsed at home, hemorrhaging from a ruptured ulcer, and very nearly died. During his convalescence, he was advised by his doctors that if he valued his life he would have to give up alcohol, and thereafter he stopped drinking permanently. Only six months after his recovery, O'Hara's wife died suddenly of a heart condition, at the age of forty-one, leaving O'Hara shattered and staring vacantly into space. With his wife's death he reached the lowest point in his life.

O'Hara had a way of making remarkable comebacks, however, and he rallied impressively after Belle O'Hara's death. In 1955, he married Katharine Barnes Bryan, whom he had known socially for a number of years. Katharine ("Sister") Bryan, divorced a year before from O'Hara's friend Joseph Bryan III, an editor at *The Saturday Evening Post*, came from a socially prominent family and was the grandniece of the industrialist W. C. Whitney and a cousin of the philanthropist John Hay ("Jock") Whitney. With his third marriage O'Hara commenced his major period, publishing eighteen volumes between 1955 and 1970, including his large novels *Ten North Frederick*, *From the Terrace*, and *Ourselves to Know*.

Ten North Frederick, set solidly in Gibbsville, was both a critical and a popular success and received the National Book Award for fiction for 1955. Two years later a second honor came to O'Hara when he was inducted into the National Institute of Arts and Letters. During the same year Katharine O'Hara opened the new house she had built on several acres five miles outside Princeton, a ten-room white brick house in the French provincial style, that the O'Haras called "Linebrook." In 1960 O'Hara, now the squire of "Linebrook," at last relented in his boycotting of *The New Yorker*. William Shawn, the *New Yorker* editor, was invited to "Linebrook," where he was shown three nouvelles, later collectively entitled *Sermons and Soda-Water*. One of them, "Imagine Kissing Pete," impressed him, and was subsequently published in *The New Yorker*, opening a new phase of O'Hara's relationship with the magazine.

For the next ten years, O'Hara's stories appeared

constantly in *The New Yorker*. Generally longer, of a different weave and texture than his earlier ones, these stories enlarged O'Hara's claim to mastery in the short story form. O'Hara published two hundred and twenty-five short stories in *The New Yorker* alone, a record that has never been approached by another writer, and in all he published more than four hundred stories. While working on his novels, O'Hara was yet able to produce new tales prolifically, a volume of them appearing almost every year. The first volume, entitled *Assembly* (1961), was followed rapidly by a series of others—*The Cape Cod Lighter* (1962), *The Hat on the Bed* (1963), *The Horse Knows the Way* (1964), *Waiting for Winter* (1966), *And Other Stories* (1968), and the posthumous volumes *The Time Element* (1972) and *Good Samaritan* (1974). Remarkably, although short story collections normally sell only modestly, O'Hara's collections enjoyed large sales. Most of his books published during this late period, in fact—both short story collections and novels became immediate best sellers. O'Hara became the most popular serious writer in America.

As a personality, O'Hara remained an eccentric in many ways, a man prone to take offense whether or not any had been intended. When his publisher, Bennett Cerf, called O'Hara on the telephone through his secretary, so that he had to wait until Cerf was put on the wire, O'Hara responded with a shocking letter informing him that as a result of the insult he was now contemplating giving his profitable novels to another publisher. Random House had its offices in the Villard mansion, and O'Hara demanded, and was given, space in the parking area before the mansion whenever he drove into New York in his Rolls-Royce, with its special license plate "JOH-1." O'Hara's display of his wealth could at times give the impression of a bounder's idea of a gentleman. One of his biographers notes that he had a gold cigarette case on which the seals of his various clubs were embossed, and he would leave it casually on a coffee table, always happy to explain what they signified. Even with his compatible marriage and comfortable circumstances, he continued to feel aggrieved. From 1964 to 1966 he contributed a column of opinion to *Newsday* in which he vented an assortment of indignations. His Tory attitudes and defense of the war in Vietnam made former friends like John Steinbeck hesitate to call on him.

One has the sense, during these years, of O'Hara's absorption with his writing in his "Linebrook" study, furnished with his trophies and honorifics. Of literary honors he received very few, the most notable of which being the Award of Merit for the Novel presented by the American Academy of Arts and Letters in 1964. The previous winners of the medal, which was awarded every five years, had been Theodore Dreiser, Thomas Mann, Ernest Hemingway, and Aldous Huxley. The one great award that O'Hara privately yearned for was the Nobel Prize. The winning of the Nobel Prize, he confided to Bennett Cerf, was a motive force of his prodigious industry since the mid-1950s. He calculated that, the prize having been given earlier to Sinclair Lewis and Ernest Hemingway, it was now time for it to go to another American. But when, in 1962, it was awarded to John Steinbeck, he saw his dream of winning the prize go up in smoke. In fact, the motive force of his ceaseless industry of this time had less to do with the prize than with more obscure currents in his psychology—his well-known fear of approaching death, and an underlying sense of inferiority or unworthiness that all his successes had not assuaged. Although he sometimes barked like a mastiff at his critics, O'Hara was a sensitive man. At the ceremony at which he was awarded the Medal of Merit, he openly wept.

In the 1960s, in addition to his other work, O'Hara

wrote a group of late novels that included *Elizabeth Appleton* (1963), an academic novel; *The Lockwood Concern* (1965), a generational saga set in "the Region"; *The Instrument* (1967), an account of the nihilistic world of a Broadway playwright; *Lovely Childs* (1969), a work dealing with the disintegration of a family belonging to Pennsylvania's Main Line society; and *The Ewings* (1970), a study of business success set against the background of personal failure. By the spring of 1970, O'Hara's health began to fail. On April 11, 1970, at "Linebrook," after beginning a new novel, *The Second Ewings*, he died in his sleep at the age of sixty-five. He left a large estate, over a million dollars having been put aside in his royalty account at Random House alone. On his tombstone (not at his direction) were inscribed the words: "Better than anyone else, he told the truth about his time, the first half of the twentieth century. He was a professional. He wrote honestly and well." O'Hara's critics cringed at the words "better than anyone else," which seemed to them typical of his vainglory. Despite many solid accomplishments in fiction, O'Hara had not usually fared well with critics, particularly with the academic establishment, which has slighted and very nearly ignored him.

There are understandable reasons that academic critics have felt uncomfortable with O'Hara's work. It does not offer a rich play of ideas to formal analysis as much modernist writing does, and it lacks political consciousness. In addition, the novels are flawed by crudeness in characterization and plotting, and are overburdened by a preoccupation with his characters' sexual lives. But O'Hara was, if judged fairly, one of the best American writers of his period. He created hundreds of characters that are living and real, and, if he could be crude, he could also be splendidly observant and subtle. His interest is largely psychological,

his vision dark but subject to many modulations suggesting complex awareness. His theme was human
loneliness and undoing, but he was also a great humorist (of an offbeat and perhaps grotesque kind), and he
had a zest for life in its myriad possibilities of embodiment in fiction. He created a world, and within the
limitations of that world, had a kind of brilliance.
O'Hara was not "better than anyone," but he was, impressively, a "professional," a prejudiced observer
who went into society and came back to record all the
terrible things he had seen.

2

The Early Short Stories: The Existential Humorist

It was as a writer of short stories that O'Hara first made his reputation. His stories began to appear in *The New Yorker* as early as 1928, but these early, apprenticeship pieces, generally brief sketches or plotless vignettes, were not included in O'Hara's first short story collection *The Doctor's Son and Other Stories* (1935), which draws chiefly from the tales he wrote between 1931 and 1934. Although distinctly O'Hara's own work, the tales in *The Doctor's Son* sometimes suggest the influence of other, established writers he admired, particularly Hemingway. Like Hemingway's tales, O'Hara's tend to be spare, reduced to stark, dramatic essentials, with characters captured quickly and concisely in hard, flat outline rather than in full dimension. Narrated with detachment and objectivity, the stories concentrate upon conflict and usually end with some kind of revelation, often understated, and achieved through the use of small naturalistic details. Hemingway is recalled especially in O'Hara's tales that depict low-life or marginal men, such as drifters or gamblers, who are powerless to control their destinies and illustrate the inescapable brutality of experience.

Compared to Hemingway, however, O'Hara reveals a more strongly developed social orientation. His characters, even at the beginning, have the most exact social definition. Whatever the characters say or do is perfectly in keeping with the social place they occupy; and they are, furthermore, always conscious of the social place of others relative to their own. A writer of considerable range, O'Hara is able to strike off hundreds of American social types, all having remarkable authenticity. But certain types appear more often than others, and O'Hara's treatment of them suggests the influence of Ring Lardner and, to a lesser degree, of Dorothy Parker. O'Hara is indebted to Lardner particularly for his scathing, poker-faced satire of average Americans whose chief characteristics are their shallowness, meanness, and need to assert themselves over others. But at times he also draws upon Lardner's narrative device of the first-person narrator who is unconscious of the extent to which he betrays his own callousness or absence of values. In other tales, O'Hara's nearly mindless characters adrift in urban settings have the styling of Dorothy Parker's *New Yorker* stories. O'Hara manages somehow to accommodate these diverse influences and to speak with a voice recognizably his own.

The Doctor's Son contains tales of various kinds, most of them first published in *The New Yorker*. The longest story in the collection, however, "The Doctor's Son," was not previously published. It is also one of O'Hara's important early achievements. Reminiscent of Hemingway's "Indian Camp," "The Doctor's Son" is an initiation story about an adolescent boy and his doctor father, and the shock of recognition that comes to the boy as he learns the meaning of adult experience. The setting is Gibbsville, the time 1918, during the outbreak of an influenza epidemic that leaves hundreds dead. It begins with a dramatic situation, as Dr. Malloy drops from exhaustion after attending the sick and dying, and a young man from a medical school in Philadelphia, called Dr. Myers, although he has not yet received his medical degree, is called in to assist. James Malloy, who is fifteen, narrates the work, and it is through his eyes that events are seen with a sharp, unflinching realism. Acting as Dr. Myers's driver, he witnesses many scenes of death, including one in a "Hunky" or Polish home where a stout, sobbing woman rocks a dead baby in her arms. In a room beyond, the body of a man who has been dead for twenty-four hours or more is suddenly discovered, and the sight causes the boy to vomit. Encountered in Collieryville, also, are a Mr. Evans, a coal-mining company superintendent, his wife, and their seventeen-year-old daughter Edith, on whom James has a crush.

While scenes of illness and death occupy part of James's attention, the interest of the work is kept focused by a set of close, very tense personal relationships—the boy's with Dr. Myers, with the members of the Evans household, and with his father. At one point he comes upon a scene in which he discovers Dr. Myers kissing Mrs. Evans, a disturbing revelation that the Evans household is not all that he had imagined it to be. In the course of the story it comes out that many things are not what they "should" be. By the end, quite unpredictably, Mr. Evans dies of influenza. That this wholly admirable man should not have been spared adds to the discrepancy that runs through the story between what ought to be and what is. Dr. Myers appears as a healer, but brings about the disruption of a family. James admires his father, an authority figure, and yet the two are at the verge of open warfare, witnessed particularly in the late scene after Dr. Malloy recovers. As James drives him to visit the sick, a violent quarrel breaks out between them. When the father speaks caustically of the boy's interest in working for a newspaper when he ought to be preparing to become a doctor, who is of use to mankind, James stops the car on the highway and threatens his father with a tire iron. A pattern of broken relationships emerges—Mrs.

Evans's betrayal of her husband; Dr. Myers's violation of the professional ethics that Dr. Malloy holds sacred; James's failed communication with his father. These broken relationships reinforce the story's encompassing irony that the terrible epidemic is ultimately contained but the forces dividing human beings cannot be.

In "The Doctor's Son," O'Hara makes no authorial comment of any kind on the incidents that occur or what they may mean; but because the story is finely crafted, everything in it is relevant. One notices, for example, that O'Hara's detailed yet concise picture of the community is ultimately a factor in the total sense of the experience portrayed. The Malloys belong to Gibbsville and its gentry class, but the action takes place almost entirely in an outlying mining village or "patch" called Collieryville, a poor area where life is lived in the rough. But here, too, social stratification can be noticed. As district superintendent of a large mining company, Mr. Evans is Collieryville's "third" citizen, after its leading doctor and leading lawyer. Below him in status are the Irish priest, the cashier of the larger of two banks, the brewer, and the leading merchant. Even at an impoverished "Hunky" house, where goats graze in a yard littered with junk, certain forms and niceties are observed—for one, the front door of the house is reserved exclusively for the use of the priest when he comes on sick calls.

At the same time, however, this social structure is somewhat makeshift and gives little sense of wholeness and harmony. Collieryville is divided ethnically, with the Irish predominant economically over the Polish, and in the saloon scenes the inhabitants of Collieryville seem like a rabble. Violence is apt to break out unpredictably. Even the fearless Dr. Malloy sleeps in his office armed with a gun, his life having been threatened by people from Collieryville who have become deranged by grief. And Dr. Malloy himself, one of the most responsible characters in the work, is capable of violence, once having struck and broken the jaw of a policeman who stopped him when he was responding to an urgent sick call. In other words, there is a functioning social order but the order it ensures is merely provisional, with an irrationality that may break out or assert itself in a way that no one can foresee. In this respect, "The Doctor's Son" is similar to *Appointment in Samarra*. In *Appointment in Samarra*, Julian English is selected, for some inscrutable reason, to be sacrificed; in "The Doctor's Son," the Evanses are destroyed as a family.

"The Doctor's Son" achieves its focus, however, and has been given unity of effect through its adolescent narrator. James is somewhat off to the side of the main incidents, but everything that happens bears upon him. What is emphasized about him is that he has reached the age to challenge his father. At fifteen, he is big for his age, physically and sexually ahead of his years, and has already angered his father by declining to become a doctor like himself. The antagonism between them is not mild, since the incident in which James brandishes the tire iron reveals a suppressed desire to murder his father. Whether an Oedipal dimension exists in the conflict between the father and son can be debated. What is certain is that James must now differentiate himself from his parent and stand by himself. But what he discovers, as the result of his exposure to disease-stricken Collieryville, is that the world is less "safe" than he had imagined. Collieryville, a raw, lower world (even in a sense a "night world"), is imperiled by death and there is no love in it. James's sexual attraction to Edith Evans leads only to estrangement. Ashamed that he shares her knowledge of her mother's familiarity with Dr. Myers, a painful experience that is compounded by the death of her father, Edith avoids him, and before long elopes with a young man. As the narrative moves at the end from the recalled past to a later point in James's experience, he remarks that he can no longer even remember Edith's married name, emphasizing further the impermanent nature of time and human relationships, and making the story not only an episode of youth but also a prophecy of adult experience.

Another story, "It Must Have Been Spring," an extension of "The Doctor's Son," concentrates upon a small incident. Its opening sentence evokes the relationship of father and son through ironic understatement: "My father's office was on the way to the stable, and we must have been at peace that day." The sentence suggests that they are not usually or often at peace, that the episode represents an intermission of strife. Skillfully, O'Hara creates the tension between the two, the boy's longing for his father's approval. Surprisingly to the boy, the father passes favorably on the appearance of his new riding outfit, and gives him a five-dollar bill, telling him to give it to his mother to put into the bank for him. The final lines capture the relationship poignantly: "'Thank you,' I said, and turned away, because suddenly I was crying. I went up the street to the stable with my head bent down, because I could let the tears roll right out of my eyes and down to the ground without putting my hand up to my face. I knew he was still looking." This ending is perfectly placed because it reveals, with the effect of a closing epiphany, what is wrong with the relationship, that it prohibits any admission or expression of tenderness.

"The Doctor's Son" and "It Must Have Been Spring" initiate a long series of stories set in Gibbsville, some of them having James Malloy as their narrator or focal character. But they are not wholly typical of the volume, since the stories in it are of various types and are set in different places, including New York and Hollywood. As a group, they have one striking common feature: they often depict characters who are essentially alone and have to cope with their isolation. In "Alone," a widower weeps by himself; in "The Man Who Had to Talk to Somebody," a middle-aged man is shunned by his wife and daughter, and loses his job; and in "Mr. Cass and the Ten Thousand Dollars," a man who lives at his club finds that even when an unexpected windfall comes to him he is still a solitary.

"Sportsmanship," set in a pool hall, has a taut, raw-edged styling in the manner of Hemingway; at the end of the brutal tale, a character named Dark breaks the protagonist's hands with a pool cue. "Pleasure," a vignette that has the stark quality of Depression realism, concerns a young Polish woman who works as a clean-up girl in a cafeteria; alone in New York, she sometimes "escapes" by going to twenty-five-cent movies, and at home hoards her meager savings and some cigarette butts. Puffing at a "whole" cigarette at the end, she experiences a moment of "pure pleasure." The story is a small study in irony, since there is no pleasure in the woman's life in any meaningful sense, and there is no one to whom she is close.

In another group of stories, O'Hara writes as an acerbic satirist, particularly when he deals with show-business people, actresses, and chorus girls. "Of Thee I Sing, Baby" depicts a chorus girl or chorine from an industrial wasteland in Queens who is near the end of her brief career in show business and beginning to go out with gangsters. It contains no authorial comment, but the title, a play on the lyrics of the hallowed national song "My Country, 'Tis of Thee," suggests the extent to which she has been formed by and reflects murky American values. What distinguishes O'Hara's satire in this story, as in others, is its harshly assaultive quality, which reduces his characters to near zombies, whether they are part of show business or belong to middle-class society.

A good illustration of O'Hara's method is the vignette-like story "New Day," which concerns a woman whose husband is a branch manager with a company in New York. She is revealed at the opening through a number of slight but telling details. As she begins her day, she brushes her teeth, which are said to be "smallish." Later, when she leaves the building and the white-haired doorman barely takes any notice of her, she reflects that "people with snow-white hair look very nice but weren't real friendly"—which suggests that she has no ability to generalize. What she is aware of are small details, noted one at a time. At a Childs restaurant, she observes that "this was a real nice waitress, and she always brought the bacon real crisp." At the end, her comic, unsigned telegram to her husband downtown, informing him that she has decided to go swimming, is the height of absurdity. Telegrams are for busy people, with timetables and schedules, but she has nothing whatever to do, and there is nothing in her life.

The ironic distance O'Hara creates between his characters' consciousness and his own superior one is also seen in "Ella and the Chinee," about an Irish girl from the Bronx, Ella O'Connor, who goes to work as a waitress in a restaurant owned by the Chinese Mr. Lee. Mr. Lee, as an "exotic" Oriental, gives Ella the "creeps," and she wonders if he takes dope—like her uncle. More pointedly, she speculates on his sexuality, wondering even if he may not have hypnotized her "so that she didn't know what was going on." In fact, it is Ella herself who seems sexually aroused. She stands in Mr. Lee's way so that he has to brush against her in order to pass by, and samples his cigarette to see if it "tasted different." She has been told by her parents that all Orientals are sinister and untrustworthy, but it is she who steals from the blameless man's cash register. Rather than making any direct comment, O'Hara merely allows the reader to note the discrepancy between Ella's perception of the situation and the situation itself.

Other stories are concerned with marriage, and range from the relatively uncomplicated "Lombard's Kick" to the more sophisticated "All the Girls He Wanted," in which the real drama of the story takes place within the wife's mind. "All the Girls He Wanted" is particularly worth noting because in this tale O'Hara allows the principal character a fuller inner dimension than he had permitted others, who serve chiefly as objects of his irony. But the finest of these marital stories, and the one giving the greatest attention to a character's inner life, is "Over the River and Through the Wood."

The protagonist of "Over the River and Through the Wood" is a Mr. Winfield, a widower in his middle sixties who makes a Thanksgiving trip with his granddaughter and two of her friends to his former house, which he has since given to his daughter and her husband. In the course of the trip, as O'Hara looks into his consciousness, his earlier life is revealed—his affair with a woman that ended when she went to live in London rather than injure his wife, his acceptance of his emotionally barren marriage that fills the story with a sense of mistake and lasting regret. The house that holds the history of his married life has a faintly symbolic quality, and it contains doors that must not be opened. Kay Farnsworth, one of his granddaughter's friends, an attractive girl who would, he thinks, know her own mind, makes him forget for a while the regret that gnaws at him. Wishing to invite her to share cocoa and biscuits with him, he knocks on the door of her bedroom, which connects with his. When he hears some muffled words on the other side, which he thinks may be "come in," or perhaps "wait a moment," he hesitates, but then opens the door—to find Kay changing her clothes and all but nude. Calling him a dirty old man, she screams at him to leave; and he returns to his room to wait for remorse to set in—for at some level of consciousness, he is not innocent. "For a while," O'Hara concludes, "he would just sit there and plan his own terror."

The Doctor's Son is an impressive short story collection, containing a large number of superior tales, including some, such as "The Doctor's Son," "It Must Have Been Spring," and "Over the River and Through the Wood," that are among O'Hara's finest. It reveals O'Hara, furthermore, in his many-sidedness—as a regional realist as well as an urban satirist, and as an explorer of modern marriage. *Files on Parade* (1939), which follows it, contains many good stories but is a somewhat slighter volume. In incorporating four stories from the *Pal Joey* cycle-in-progress and two tales from the earlier collection, it gives the impression that O'Hara may have been pressed to fill out a new volume, timed to follow and take advantage of the publication of his novel *Hope of Heaven*. Like *Hope of Heaven*, it shows a newly developed interest in the special world of Hollywood, where seven of the stories are set.

"I Could Have Had a Yacht" is essentially a monologue, narrated by a type O'Hara had created in *The Doctor's Son*, the show girl. She is revealed by her own words, her poses, her pretension to superior standards. What makes her vivid particularly is O'Hara's uncanny ear for American speech, which in her case contains a preposterous mixture of refinement and vulgarity:

Like he said to me on the way home in the taxi. He was sitting there with a cigar in his mouth and not even condescending to hold up his end of the conversation except yes or no once in a while, then all of a sudden he said, "Say, Toots, you have a nice pair of gams." "Oh," I said. "I have a nice pair of gams," I said to him. "Aren't you the old eagle eye, though?" "You been to the show three nights in succession, if one is to believe your story," I said, "and," I said, "just now you notice my nice legs. Where were you looking if you're just finding that out?" I said. "Mr. Carroll thinks so, too, and so do a lot of other people that I'd take their word for it sooner than I would yours. Where were you looking at the time?" "Not at your legs," he said.

But this acidulous portrait pales before that of the Hollywood actress in "Most Gorgeous Thing," cast in the form of a self-justifying monologue. The movie queen narrator relates to her friend Lucille the story of her relationship with Eddie MacIllaney, who regards her as the only friend he has left in the world. She finds him a job at her studio paying barely forty dollars a week, writing adaptations of classics that will never be used but are necessary in order to hold copyright; and while engaged in this pointless work he becomes more alcoholically despondent. Sometimes at four in the morning, if she is vaguely depressed, she calls him on the telephone and has him come to her house to cheer her up. On one of these occasions, he attempts to make love to her, but she rebuffs him, telling him that she cannot feel about him "in that way." Yet she has him accompany her in her pool where she swims in the nude—seemingly unaware that she is inciting his hopeless infatuation.

When Eddie becomes gravely ill, his doctor asks her to help him, since he will die if he continues to drink. Piqued by the implication that his heavy drinking may have to do with her, she is curt with the doctor and refuses to answer MacIllaney's calls. When he commits suicide, the actress does not even go to the funeral home since, as she explains to Lucille, "I can't bear to look at a dead person." O'Hara takes some risks with this movie queen, pushing her self-centeredness to an extreme; yet in a certain way she is credible, her vanity and lack of feeling having been nurtured, after all, by a world in which artificial values prevail.

O'Hara's actresses, however, with their self-concern and painfully limited natures, are not unlike other characters who appear in his tales that have nothing to do with show business. In the frequency of their appearance and their meanness of spirit, these characters suggest O'Hara's own contemptuous view of humanity. In stories like "Ice Cream," the characters play a game of one-upmanship, putting others down so that they may think better of themselves. "Ice Cream" is set in New York during a sweltering summer that simmers with frustration. Its constricted setting is a small hotel room, to which Harry, the principal character, brings a container of ice cream (the wrong flavor) to his heavy wife, who calls him a "dope."

His wife is a "big mound" of a woman who, as she is first seen, lies on a bed smoking a cigarette. "Her fingers and breasts were small," O'Hara remarks, "but the flesh rolled down on the backs of her hands and over her ankles, and under the black net negligee she was huge in the hips and abdomen and thighs." As she lies on the bed like a grotesquely parodic version of a sex goddess, a strangely diminutive dog looks up at her quizzically. In the heavy, torpid atmosphere of this room, Harry tells his wife about his having just encountered on the street her first husband, a musician now out of work. With obvious satisfaction, he recounts how he not only refused him an insignificantly small loan but also humiliated him sharply. One's sense of the pettiness of his triumph over the other man is increased by the presence of his obese wife, who mocks the idea of romantic rivalry and is a reminder that Harry, too, is one of the defeated. Characters like Harry give the impression that O'Hara's sense of society consists of nothing more than the nastiness and bad temper of individuals who can hardly bear their lives.

A jewellike story, about the cruelty latent in human nature, is "Olive." At a quiet residential hotel in New York, Colonel Browder, a seventy-year-old man recently widowed, begins having afternoon tea with a new tenant, a Miss Bishop, thirty years younger than he, a shy, unmarried woman who has no friends. Their having afternoon tea together becomes an enjoyable ritual in their sparsely furnished lives; and then one day one of the hotel switchboard operators, Olive, begins to make cutting remarks about their "little romance." When Miss Bishop attempts to make out-of-hotel phone calls, Olive is so rude to her that she finally decides to live elsewhere. The colonel continues to have afternoon tea, hoping that Miss Bishop may return, but he does not see her again. What is disturbing in the story is the mysterious and unmotivated nature of Olive's spiteful act, her venomous assault upon the gentle and innocent.

A group of stories in *Files on Parade* deal with the manners of more worldly characters. These include the ironic "Saffercisco," set in Hollywood, and "Lunch Tuesday," which takes place at an East Side restaurant in New York. Both are skillfully crafted and deal with infidelity in marriage, but another tale, "Days," has particular interest since it shows O'Hara extending this theme to the suburbs. In its suburban setting and somewhat dreamlike atmosphere, it gives the impression that it might have been written by John Cheever. In "Days," a well-to-do suburbanite named Larkin is driven by his wife each morning to the local railroad station, where he takes the commuter train into New York. On the way to the station, always at the same time, he notices an attractive young woman come out of her building, and he later glimpses her aboard the train. One day he engages a chauffeur to work for him so that he will not be seen by this woman, about whom he has begun to fantasize, when his wife kisses him goodbye. Not long afterward, he is on the train, and as he thinks of the strange nature of his situation, he suddenly laughs aloud. The woman, then seated in front of him, turns to look at him with a smile; and as she does, his fantasy and real life begin strangely to merge.

What is striking about "Days," compared to many other stories in the volume, is that it takes place to a large extent within the mind of the principal character. The same is true of "The Cold House," in which a woman from New York, a Mrs. Carnavon, makes a visit to a house she owns in the country but has not been to for some time; she seems drawn to it reluctantly and against her will. The house is maintained for her by two servants. However, when she arrives, there are no fires in the fireplaces and the house is cold. In the chilly house it begins to become clear that Mrs. Carnavon is a wealthy widow with a problem. Upstairs in the house, Mrs. Carnavon finds it difficult to look at her son's room, which she had considered having permanently locked. She tells herself, "Just let him be dead," but knows that she cannot remove her son from her thoughts by locking a door. What happened between them in the past is made all the more evocative, as in certain stories of Henry James, by its never being specified. One can only say that she has returned under a compulsion to a house that belongs to her but that she cannot live in, and has now reached an impasse. She must go on hating a memory "she only knew how to love."

One feature of "The Cold House" that is unusual for O'Hara at this point in his career is that the house has a symbolic connotation, is the outward embodiment of Mrs. Carnavon's inner conflict. The psychological orientation of the story and use of the house as a symbolic framing device, in fact, look forward to such later novels as *Ten North Frederick, Ourselves to*

Know, and *The Lockwood Concern*. The introspective quality of "The Cold House," and to a degree of "Days," gives a certain ambivalence to the *Files on Parade* collection. It suggests other directions in the short story that are available to O'Hara besides the ones that predominate in the volume—the spare, naturalistic study of characters who are perceived in their externals and are frequently deprived of consciousness.

Limited consciousness is what one notices immediately in Joey Evans, the hero, or more properly anti-hero, of *Pal Joey* (1940), which followed *Files on Parade* by only a year. The stories making up the volume are composed in the form of a series of fourteen letters written by Joey, a small-time nightclub singer, to his friend Ted, a more successful entertainer in New York, but these letters are actually monologues—in which Joey reveals more about himself than he realizes. O'Hara's method in the letters is similar to (and fairly obviously inspired by) Ring Lardner's in *You Know Me Al*, about a Chicago baseball player; and like Lardner's hero, Joey fractures the English language, misspells words, and generally betrays a comic illiteracy. By the end of the volume, the reader comes to feel that he knows Joey thoroughly—and the dim, déclassé world he comes out of.

Pal Joey is enlivened by O'Hara's street-wise sense of life, his ability to mimic nightclub operators, bouncers, "dames," and the various other denizens of a nocturnal world; and it is made particularly vivid through O'Hara's ear for speech. Joey so handles the language that "educated" and vernacular speech come together in improbable combinations, as in this passage from an early story in the collection:

First of all the ass't mgr. of the hotel where I am singing he comes to me and says "Joey I just rec'd information that is not doing you any good around this town. . . . We are both men of the world but this is what I have reference to, meaning that a certain mouse from this town had to leave town on acc't of you. . . . That don't do you any good personally and I will state frankly that while we are highly pleased with your singing and drawing power here at the hotel however we have to look at [it] [*sic*] from all the angles and once it gets around that you are the kind of chap that writes letters to his pals in N.Y. mentioning his fatal attraction to the ladies why some nite some guy is just going to get his load on and you are singing and a guy will walk up and take a poke at you while you are singing. Think it over," he said.

The confusion of polite and street English in Joey's letters is more than comic, since it keeps Joey's obsession with success, impossible of attainment, constantly before the reader. He aspires to social acceptability, but is continually brought down to a recognition of his placelessness. He prides himself on his appeal to women, but his masculinity seems in question, since he is powerless to manage his life. To Joey, a woman, whom he calls a "mouse," is prey; but Joey is in turn prey to everyone else, including women, like Jean Benedict in "Joey at the Calcutta Club." They are cannier and stronger-willed than he is. In *Pal Joey*, O'Hara envisions a jungle world in which the most unscrupulous survive best, where appearances are deceptive and no one, man or woman, can be trusted. Comparatively speaking, Joey is by no means the worst of the characters in the volume; he is merely ill-equipped to survive. In "Bow Wow," he tells an unsophisticated stenographer that when his people lost their money in the crash he had to leave Princeton to go to work; and while it is amusing that she believes his story, what the tale reveals, sadly, is the deprivation of his past, matching the deprivation of any future that can be imagined for him.

Pal Joey can be read as a humorous account of a rogue at loose in a world, an account with the cartoon-like quality of Damon Runyon's Broadway tales. But the Joey story cycle is more genuinely absurdist than anything in Runyon; its humor has an intellectual quality, indeed, that evokes bitter, complex awareness. When Joey writes his final letter to "Pal Ted," he reveals how much he resents and hates this only "friend"— how totally, pitifully alone he is. Joey may be likable to a degree, but he does not like himself, and his imagination has an obsessional quality. He seems locked into his deprivations, his muteness, denied any hope of grace or salvation. In a way that may be funny but is also sinister, Joey Evans is one of O'Hara's paralyzed male characters, who have only a questionable masculinity to protect them from the threat of life.

The threat of life is pervasive in *Pipe Night* (1945), in which O'Hara writes as an objective and unsparing naturalist. The volume's typically brief tales, written during World War II, are minimalist in statement and markedly pessimistic in mood. One story in particular, "Nothing Missing," suggests the nature of the others. In "Nothing Missing," a clerk, a young woman named Miss White, opens the gift shop where she works one morning and before long a man comes in to browse. He talks strangely, and there is something about him that is disturbing. His remarks are terse, odd, and somewhat unnerving. Finally he mentions that he has just come out of prison. He tries to talk to Miss White but she is frightened and, pretending to be writing a letter, she ignores him until he finally leaves, exclaiming, "What the hell kind of a life is this, anyway?" She then walks around the shop where he had browsed, but is reassured that nothing is missing. The irony of the story, however, is that something *is* missing—in Miss White's own life, hemmed in with little anxieties and a small, boring job. Something is missing, too, in the life of the ex-convict, whose arrogance in the shop turns quickly to defeat. And something is missing, finally, in their attempt to communicate. As in Hem-

ingway's story "Hills Like White Elephants," nothing is
stated overtly, but through externals and understated
details a whole sense of life is evoked.

A number of the tales take place during World
War II but, reflecting O'Hara's own noncombatant
role during the war, they are set on the home front.
What they reveal is the alienation of many lives. In
"Platform," an attempted pickup on a train between a
sailor and a young woman ends in rancor and name
calling; and in "The Lieutenant," a returning war hero
finds that he is now estranged from his old companions. Nor is there harmony when servicemen return on
furlough to their wives and families. In "Leave," a sailor
is first struck in the face by his father and then involved in a barroom fracas; he has come back to confront relationships in which there is only hostility or incoherence. In "Patriotism," a soldier on leave returns
to a wife who is having an affair with another man.
Her lover feels guilty that she will not sleep with her
husband even on his last night home, but the wife, who
is without qualms, tells him that he is a "goddam
patriot."

In other, less assaultive stories, O'Hara's characters are typically at the mercy of life, and are forced to
confront their isolation and loneliness. In "Summer's
Day," one of the volume's finest tales, Mr. and Mrs. Attrell, an older couple, are spending a day at a local
beach. A certain habitualness, suggesting a need for
order in their lives, is noticeable at the beginning, as
can be seen in the boardwalk bench they occupy that
has a little marker, "A. T. Attrell," nailed on its back. A
Mr. O'Donnell, a war veteran and former athlete who
has come to the beach with his boys, greets the Attrells
respectfully. All is as it should be. Then Mr. Attrell,
deciding that he would like to take a dip, goes to the
bathhouse to change. While he is changing in his booth
(marked "A. T. Attrell"), he overhears some boys

commenting on him and his wife as "the local tragedy," the couple whose daughter hanged herself in the stable over a love affair. Then the voice of Mr. O'Donnell is heard, as he smacks one of the boys and tells them to get out. Inside the booth, Attrell wonders how he can ever face Henry O'Donnell again, only to recognize that there is "nothing to face." The Attrells' future is a blank.

The sense of entrapment experienced by Attrell appears at many points in *Pipe Night*, but in one tale, "A Respectable Place," in a particularly disturbing way. "A Respectable Place" concerns a bar owner in New Haven named Matty Wall, whose last name is like a clue to his situation. A wall, after all, indicates a spatial limitation, and suggests the idea of confinement or enclosure. Wall, in any case, is a decent man who makes an honest living and keeps a "respectable" place. Then one day a policeman named Roy Morley comes in and, because he knows him only too well, Matty begins to feel uneasy. Earlier, Morley had been mixed up in bootlegging, protected by his uncle, the chairman of the State Republican Committee, who also arranged to have him appointed to the police department. Morley is the type of man who may drink all day without showing his inebriation and then, suddenly, become an ugly, fighting drunk.

After he has begun to drink at the bar, Morley pulls out his revolver, puts its barrel into his mouth, and pulls the trigger. The trigger clicks, and nothing happens. He then begins shooting out the bar mirrors, and hurls his bottle of rye at a row of bottles along the back bar. The following morning a police lieutenant stops by to ask how much money will be needed to cover the damages, but the incident does not end here. The police begin to put pressure on Matty Wall, issuing summonses, although they had never done so before, for beer trucks that make deliveries at his bar and sup-

posedly obstruct traffic. When Matty attempts to ap-
pease the police by making a donation to the Police
Benevolent Fund, for the same amount as the damages
caused by Morley, it is rejected with hostility as a
"bribe." At the end, Wall is forced to close his bar.
What is conspicuous in "A Respectable Place" is its ab-
surdism; a man who has done nothing wrong suddenly
finds himself powerless before vested authority, which
has no relation to right or wrong or to justice or ration-
ality of any kind. The vision of the story encompasses
the experience of other characters in *Pipe Night,* who
find themselves shorn of importance or identity.

In contrast to *Pipe Night, Hellbox* (1947) contains
a few glimpses of brightness if not of hope. Some of
the tales are humorous, and in a way that does not lac-
erate the character depicted. "Common Sense Should
Tell You," about a Hollywood producer who is enjoy-
ing the diversions of a Chicago nightclub and the
prospect of an intimate evening with a young chorine
just as he remembers his acute heart condition, is superbly realized. So, too, is "Conversation in the
Atomic Age," in which James Malloy visits a Los Angeles society lady whose extraordinary preoccupation
with automobiles, which will take her to different places
with different sets of people, evokes the frivolous nature of her life.

In general, the stories in *Hellbox* reveal a breadth
and range that had been somewhat constricted in *Pipe
Night.* They are set variously in Pennsylvania towns,
coastal resorts of the Northeast, New England, Chicago, Hollywood, and New York. Some of O'Hara's
characters are involved with the mob, and in one tale a
young man attempts to hide out from it. Middle-class
couples are revealed through the nature of their marriages. Fathers and sons come together as strangers.
Ugly tensions simmer at late-night gatherings or at the
reunion of former friends. But the dominant theme of

Hellbox is the approach of middle age. In "Transaction," James Malloy acquires a stylish, secondhand Duesenberg from a financially hard-pressed student couple with a small child; but the youthful insouciance the auto brings to mind is no longer recoverable by Malloy, who has now passed forty. Malloy appears again in "Miss W.," as if to emphasize the point. At an Eastern girls' school he is reunited with Amy Woodberry, once an old flame but now a hard-working schoolmistress who worries about the romantic entanglement of one of her charges; and they try to tell themselves that they do not mind being middle-aged. In "Clara," a man named Dixon returns to his home town to attend to the settlement of his mother's estate, and there meets a woman named Clara whom he had once wanted to marry. She has recently been widowed, her husband having been killed in a hunting accident that is rumored to have been a suicide. Having had to step down in the world, Clara now works as a head waitress in a local restaurant. Over a drink at the restaurant, they reminisce and the old affair for a moment is revived—until Clara tells Dixon that, no matter what its outcome, she had married the right man, after all. At the end, like many of O'Hara's characters, Dixon seems unlikely to experience any measurable personal fulfillment.

It would be difficult to reduce the large number of tales contained in O'Hara's five early short story collections to a single general idea; but the absence of fulfillment is a theme that runs through a great number of them. His characters are usually balked in one way or another; they cannot establish contact with others, and thus live and die essentially alone. Some of O'Hara's characters are so lacking in consciousness that they do not have to confront their inner emptiness—although it is no less real. Those who have consciousness are likely to discover the terrible nature of life and to be robbed of any sense of importance they thought they had. In many of these tales O'Hara has a special affinity with Hemingway, whose taut, understated studies in maiming and isolation establish a tradition for him.

A crucial difference between them is that O'Hara's stories typically take place within a closely specified social context, which is never incidental to what occurs and is sometimes a determinant in the outcome of events. An irony in O'Hara's social awareness, however, is that society as he envisions it provides almost no nourishment for his characters' lives. It is marked by meanness and cruelty and is the force behind his characters' aggression and suppressed hostility. Rather than having a civilizing effect, it often blunts the characters' natures and dehumanizes them. If the early stories reveal any limitation in range, it is that O'Hara can conceive of society in almost no way other than as a mechanism in which his characters are caught and maimed. A somewhat different sense of society appears in the later stories, in which O'Hara becomes a more relaxed observer of society, which contains pleasure as well as pain and is the agency through which some of his characters come to finer awareness or larger understanding. At the point *Hellbox* marks, O'Hara is still a "young master" who has brought the short story in a certain mode to a high perfection; who has become the leading American short story writer of his generation—an ironist or existential humorist of baffled fulfillment.

3

O'Hara the Novelist: First Flight—*Appointment in Samarra*

O'Hara's first novel, *Appointment in Samarra* (1934), was written at a critical point in his life and during a time of emotional upheaval. In the early summer of 1933, Helen Petit O'Hara obtained a divorce in Reno, while O'Hara sank ever deeper into heavy drinking and despondency. At the beginning of the summer he went to work for a newspaper in Pittsburgh, but left several months later for New York where, in his bedroom at the Pickwick Arms Hotel, he began work on *Appointment in Samarra*. Up until that time his only attempt at a novel had been the fragmentary "The Hofmann Estate," written in 1931. The fragment, however, may have provided some of the material for *Appointment in Samarra*.

Some associations of a personal and literary nature entered into the writing of the novel, the working title of which was "The Infernal Grove." Midway in its composition, O'Hara called on his friend Dorothy Parker, and the visit resulted in O'Hara's deciding on the novel's final title. Miss Parker showed him a volume by Somerset Maugham containing the play *Sheppey*, which begins with a speech by Death who describes to Sheppey the futile attempt of another man to elude her by fleeing to Samarra. "I was astonished to see him in

Baghdad," Death comments, "for I had an appointment
with him in Samarra." O'Hara was so struck by this
passage that he adopted *Appointment in Samarra* as
his title—thus emphasizing the unavoidability of Julian
English's fate. Another writer who figured in the background of the novel was F. Scott Fitzgerald. By the
time O'Hara began to write the work he had formed a
friendship with Fitzgerald, who obliged O'Hara by
reading the final draft of *Appointment in Samarra*. His
judgment of it is supposed to have been "Yes-yes-but-
also-no," a reaction predicting the novel's reception
upon publication. A number of readers were shocked
by the coarseness and the sexual frankness of O'Hara's
realism, but in general the novel was acclaimed. At the
age of thirty, while living in near destitution in New
York, O'Hara suddenly found himself famous.

The personal background is relevant to *Appointment in Samarra* in other respects as well. In a letter
written in the 1960s, O'Hara identified his source for
Julian English as a man named William ("Birsie")
Richards, who took his life in Pottsville on February 14,
1933. Richards did not belong to the country club set,
but was a man who "had charm and a certain kind of
native intelligence, and who, when the chips were
down, shot himself." O'Hara "covered him up" with
Brooks Brothers clothes and a Cadillac dealership, but
"took his life, his psychological pattern"; if *Appointment in Samarra* seems real, O'Hara remarked in the
letter, it is partly because its hero comes "out of life."[1]
This source-from-life, however, does not account entirely for Julian English, who has many resemblances
to O'Hara himself. Julian's relationship to his doctor
father is similar to O'Hara's relationship to his. In both
cases, the relationship involves some distance between
father and son, a sense of the older man's disappointment in his son who had turned down the opportunity
to take up a medical career and does not have a strong
sense of direction. As an expression of disapproval, Dr.

English sends Julian not to an Eastern Ivy League college such as Yale but to Lafayette; in O'Hara's case his
father had put him on probation before deciding
whether he would go to college at all.

Moreover, Julian's relationship to his wife is as intense and ultimately as unfortunate as O'Hara's to
Helen Petit. Julian is unduly suspicious that his wife
may prefer another man in the same way that O'Hara
was suspicious of his wife's interest in other men.
These suspicions, at least partly, lead Julian to drink, to
behave unreasonably, and to make scenes, as they had
with O'Hara. O'Hara knew personally what Julian's
self-destructive behavior and desperation felt like.
This is not to say that O'Hara can be equated simply
with Julian English, or that *Appointment in Samarra*
can be accounted for entirely in autobiographical
terms. Although O'Hara understands Julian's psychology, he is also removed from him, writes with a detachment from everything, sparing no one and yet keeping
in his heart, as Dorothy Parker remarked, "a curious
and bitter mercy."

The "voice" of *Appointment in Samarra* is that of
an omniscient narrator, detached from all his characters and yet able, when occasion requires it, to search
their inmost thoughts. With the most remarkable ease
and suppleness, scenes of action alternate with episodes that reveal the flow of the characters' consciousness. The assurance in O'Hara's control over his material is apparent also in the masterful montagelike
technique of his narration.[2] In the early and late sections particularly, the chapters are broken into diverse
episodes that yet achieve a unity of effect through
O'Hara's use of ongoing time and contextual motifs.

The opening chapter, for example, begins with
the Flieglers in the bedroom of their Lantenengo
Street house; it shifts to the country club where Julian
throws a drink in the face of the Irish parvenu Harry
Reilly; and ends with Al Grecco as he cruises Gibbs-

ville, quintessentially alone, in his car. These characters are defined immediately by the social stations they
occupy. The Flieglers are a middle-class couple who
have managed to own a house on the town's best
street; and in her late-night reveries Irma Fliegler reveals her anxiety that the Brombergs, who have recently bought a house on the street, may encourage
other Jewish families to move there and thus lower the
Flieglers' own status. When Julian English appears
in the next sequence, he is seen in the inner sanctum
of the country club, its smoking room, once reserved
for the club's elite but now becoming available to almost everyone. Julian belongs to the "established" old
guard, as Al Grecco, who appears in the following sequence, is part of the town's underworld and low life.
Although differently placed, these characters have
lives that are closely interwoven. Lute Fliegler sells
cars for Julian, and Al Grecco delivers to the English
house the bootleg booze that Julian has procured from
Ed Charney.

Through panels of narration that alternate swiftly,
background information is provided obliquely rather
than being directly stated, and the concerns of one set
of characters flow into the consciousness of the next.
Irma Fliegler hears a sound below in the street—the
broken tire chain of a car banging against one of its
fenders, as their neighbors, Dr. Newton (the dentist)
and his wife, return home from the country club; looking at her husband's watch, she fixes the time at twenty
minutes past three in the morning. Irma's thoughts turn
to the country club, which the Flieglers are not yet
eligible to join, and to the Englishes, who are
members. At this moment, the narrative, with the effect of a camera cut, shifts to the country club itself,
where the focal figure is Julian English; and as with
Irma much of what occurs in this segment takes place
in his mind. Only at the end of this section, and by a

fine stroke taking place "off stage," does it come out that Julian has thrown a highball in Harry Reilly's face. The segment is followed by the appearance of Al Grecco, who also muses on his place in the world around him, and passes the country club gates just as the English car speeds hurriedly away. He follows the car to the English house, where he watches Julian and Caroline go inside and the lights go on in their upstairs bedroom. He then drives off shouting an obscenity at the slumbering residents of Lantenengo Street who have snubbed him. The whole chapter is filled with antagonism and confrontation, and it ends with an acrimonious outburst. It foreshadows Julian's fall, and it sets forth the special world O'Hara is to deal with—a world viewed from ever-shifting angles and kept under intense pressure.

The next chapter begins on Christmas day with the early morning estrangement at breakfast of Julian and Caroline; moves to the late-morning scene between the Flieglers, in which they speak of their plan to have their Christmas dinner at two P.M.; and concludes with the long, extraordinary scene in which Al Grecco has his two P.M. dinner at the dingy Apollo restaurant run by a Greek named Poppas. This episode foreshadows the later one in which the Flieglers spend Christmas evening at the Stage Coach Inn, where Julian will create a scene by becoming too familiar with Helene Holman, Ed Charney's mistress—an incident that raises the frustration of many of the characters to an unbearable level. In this manner, characters are captured in their separateness and convergence, and the work assumes the shape of the "mosaic" or pattern novel.

Following the Stage Coach incident, Julian is shown at his office plunged in remorse; Caroline lies in bed filled with anger at Julian for his humiliation of her with the Holman woman; and Al Grecco is subjected to a tirade of abuse by his boss. Everyone's nerves are on

edge, especially Julian's, and as he attempts to find relief in alcohol, his erratic behavior merely increases
until he "escapes" at last, irreversibly, by taking his life.
The final chapter is narrated in fragments that record
the shocked aftermath of Julian's death, and the novel
ends as it began with the Flieglers, the middle-class
couple who are touched by but a little removed from
Julian's tragedy. Order is restored, and life, apparently,
returns to "normal." Yet in this ending, there is also a
suggestion that Julian's tragedy is more than purely
personal; that these final three days of his life have exposed the inner life and psychic stresses of his
community.

In *Appointment in Samarra*, O'Hara refers specifically to two other American writers, Fitzgerald and
Hemingway, both of whom have affected the novel's
styling. Although O'Hara elsewhere claimed Fitzgerald
specifically as an influence on the novel,[3] the reader
might wonder what he had exactly in mind. There is
nothing whatever in the work resembling the gossamer
world of romance that Fitzgerald creates in his novels.
If anything, Fitzgerald's cotillion balls have been
scaled down harshly to the spareness of Depression
realism. Yet there is a sense in which Fitzgerald is reflected in *Appointment in Samarra*, since *The Great
Gatsby* provides a model of a kind for O'Hara's narrative method. In the opening chapters of *The Great
Gatsby*, Fitzgerald depicts three distinctly different
social spheres—the established world of East Egg; the
upwardly mobile nouveaux riches of West Egg; and the
raw, anomalous, and "corrupt" world of New York City.
In the course of the work, the characters who are defined by the different social levels to which they belong
intermingle—with disastrous consequences. *Appointment in Samarra* uses an essentially similar technique,
alerting the reader immediately to the social position
of the Englishes, who stand at or near the top; the

Flieglers, who are middle class but are inching upward;
and the Al Greccos, who belong to local gangsterism.
Like *The Great Gatsby*, *Appointment in Samarra* uses a
fragmented narration that shifts from one social setting
to another so that a kaleidoscopic effect is achieved
while at the same time a sense of doom steadily develops. In both novels, the protagonists are damned, and
within the context of an existing American social
structure.[4]

The influence of Hemingway on *Appointment in
Samarra* is perhaps more immediately discernible.
Appointment in Samarra can by no means be called
imitation Hemingway, however, its relation to him
being more nearly a matter of a somewhat distant
derivation,[5] of occasional influence on styling that can
be detected. O'Hara's sinister surfaces and the economy of his prose effects (in which a vast amount about
a character and his situation is conveyed in a few
words) have a kinship with Hemingway, and particularly whenever O'Hara uses this incisive technique to
portray characters who have been hardened by life. In
an early scene, for example, Al Grecco is captured
with a terse grotesqueness, which manages to suggest
his lack of identity through his having been given an
identity that is purely of "type." "Al placed his coat on
a hanger and removed his hat," O'Hara writes of him,
"using both hands in taking off his hat so as not to dis-
turb his hair." He is as strongly "typed" here as the two
men in Hemingway's story "The Killers."

The scene at the Apollo restaurant is at once sinister and comic, and the characters who appear there
are brought to life suddenly, through the use of very
few words. The owner, for example, is presented in
the following way: "George Poppas was standing behind the cigar counter. . . . George leaned with his fat
hands folded, supporting himself on the cigar counter,
and appearing to be in great pain. George always ap-

peared to be in great pain, as though he had eaten, an hour ago, all the things that can give you indigestion. Al once had seen him in a crap game make fifteen straight passes and win over twelve thousand dollars, but he still appeared to be in great pain." Another character, the waiter, is also revealed in sharply focused externals. Because of his jug ears, which are about a third the length of his face, he is known as "Loving Cup," and the conversation between Loving Cup and Al is rendered in tough, Hemingwayesque dialogue:

> "I'll have that a dollar and a half dinner."
> "What kind of soup you want?"
> "I don't want any soup," said Al.
> "It goes with the dinner, so you don't have to pay extra. I'll bring you the cream of tomato. I just seen the chef spit in it." He jumped away as Al reached out for him.

O'Hara has furnished Al with a suitably sordid background. Growing up as Tony Murascho, he has been put out of parochial school at fourteen for striking a nun, was once arraigned for stabbing a colleague in a poolroom argument, and was later sent to the county jail for burgling a church poorbox. At eighteen, he trains under Packy McGovern as a prizefighter, and because of a female reporter's comparing his performance in the ring to the art of El Greco, he is given the nickname Al Grecco—a name that serves as a constant reminder of his debasement of ideals. Al Grecco functions as a point of contact with the lower element of Gibbsville, is familiar with its pool halls and whorehouses, and is an underling of Ed Charney's in his bootlegging and numbers operations. Through him one is introduced to Foxie Lebrix, who manages the Stage Coach roadhouse and speaks excitedly in a stream of obscene epithets, separated by a repetition of the article "a"; and to Helene Holman, Ed Charney's vacant, alcoholic mistress who performs as a torch singer. And through him, one is introduced to Ed Charney himself, the mobster who at one point excoriates Al Grecco over the telephone for having failed to keep an eye on Helene—a tirade Charney delivers, apparently, in front of his own wife and small child. Charney has been given a solid actuality, and one of the most impressive features of O'Hara's handling of him is that, while his presence is always felt, he never actually appears. He is created entirely through the consciousness of Al Grecco.

This substratum of society is never extraneous to the characters who are more highly placed socially. It represents a reality from which they are unable to divorce themselves. A mayoral candidate and many of the state police have been corrupted by Charney; and many leading citizens of Gibbsville have been known to frequent the Dew Drop brothel or to have conducted extramarital affairs at Dutch hotels beyond the town. Lip service is paid to the "noble experiment" of Prohibition, but everyone drinks illicitly, and many of them, like Julian English, drink heavily. Their claim to standing above or apart from this subterranean life is constantly negated by their implication in it, and their own authenticity is questioned.

Life at the top ought to provide a sanctuary of a kind for those able to claim membership, but it does not. As much as do the members of the lower groups, the elitist characters live under the observation of others, and their transgressions are duly noted, to be used against them eventually. Each character waits to have such a check delivered, to be humiliated and brought down. When Julian throws a drink in Harry Reilly's face, word of the incident spreads almost instantly across the town; and the Englishes become suddenly accountable to the Irish Catholics (as well as to the Catholic Poles) for a provocative act that has been directed at one of their own. A loss of business is threatened for Julian at his auto dealership, and at the country club he will be if not actually "out" then at least no longer so securely "in." He discovers that his sense of possessing an autonomous identity, the capacity to act or express himself freely, is an illusion. For his identity, like that of all the other characters, is merely conditional. He is never free to detach himself from his relative place within a social structure, and when his place within that structure collapses, he sits in a car filling with carbon monoxide fumes until "no one could have helped him, no one in the world."

O'Hara's vividly precise notation of social structures has been commented on by Edmund Wilson, who has written that to read O'Hara "on a fashionable bar or the Gibbsville country club is to be shown on the screen of a fluoroscope gradations of social prestige of which one had not before been aware."[6] One of O'Hara's special gifts is the minute exactitude with which he observes his characters as social beings. The very cars they drive set them apart and identify them (Julian significantly has a Cadillac while Lute Fliegler has only a Studebaker). The members of the country club are all socially ranked—in ways that are unstated but understood by all. Ultimately these characters are encapsulated by their arbitrary social identities.

What comes out in chapter four, to which the Ammermann dinner dance is devoted, is the boringly predictable and artificial nature of the country club's social rituals. For dinner party hosts, for example, there are never more than three menu options, arranged on the scale of the dollar-fifty dinner, the two-dollar dinner, and the two-fifty dinner. The Ammermanns, who have a new-money uncertainty, go all the way and order the top menu. Ammerman is described as a drunken roué, quite rich in real estate, and nominally a cigar manufacturer. His daughter Mildred, in whose honor the dinner is given, is a tall, toothy girl who is captain of the women's golf team. In New York, O'Hara comments, "she would have been marked as a Lesbian on sight," but in Gibbsville "was just a healthy girl."

On the dance floor an unvarying protocol is observed. If one of the "sad birds" comes with a man from out of town, the local men go out of their way to dance with her twice—to give the impression that she is popular and to boost her matrimonial chances. Once married, to any man whomsoever providing he is not a Jew, it will be politely forgotten that she has been a "sad bird," and she will take her place among the popular women. At the Ammermann dinner, Julian is seated between a "sad bird" and an attractive girl. "Always the attractive men," O'Hara writes, "or those who were accepted as attractive in Gibbsville, were given a sad bird as a duty and an attractive girl as a reward." Julian knows in advance what his seating arrangement will be, because it will be what it has been ever since he can remember. The dinner dance is symptomatic of a claustrophobic world of empty forms, and of lurking, subterranean disgust. It is in this setting that Julian discharges his disgust on Harry Reilly.

His anger is the anger of the man who has no real identity; has only the identity furnished him by his cooperation with a system of hierarchical arrangements and codes of behavior having no authenticity. It could be said that Julian strikes out at Reilly, who has bought his way into the inner sanctum of the country club, because he is a reminder to him that his own life may be inauthentic or valueless. In Reilly, he sees the dubiousness of his existence, upon which his mind has begun to dwell. Does his wife really love him? Is she having an affair with another man? Why instead of serving with honor overseas did he spend the war years in college? Why has his father, Dr. English, given him so little respect and shown him so little love? Julian lashes out at everything that threatens him, but by doing so, by defying tacitly agreed-upon social codes, he upsets what equilibrium there has been in his life, which begins to turn into a nightmare.

He is not alone, however, in the uncertainty he shows of his identity. O'Hara's characters have been given sharp definition of a kind by the jobs they hold, the amount of income they earn, the street on which they live, the colleges they attended, the clubs to which they do or do not belong. But otherwise they inhabit a spiritual vacuum. In order to shore up their very tenuous sense of self, they are ever ready to strike out at others, to raise themselves up by putting others down. At the breakfast table, Lute Fliegler pretends to read to his wife a newspaper article reporting that Marvyn Schwartz, a Gibbsville neighbor, has been shot and killed in a brothel on Christmas Eve. It is a joke, but clearly it implies an embitterment and lurking aggression in Lute.

Once this aggressive impulse is acted upon, it spreads with a ripple effect through the town. On Christmas morning, suffering the frustration of his loss of status, Julian speaks rudely to his housekeeper, Mrs. Grady; and during the same day, having also lost face, Ed Charney furiously rebukes Al Grecco. Mrs. Grady and Al Grecco then confront each other when Grecco makes his delivery of Scotch whiskey at the English house, and they exchange remarks meant to denigrate and humiliate each other, to shatter the other's sense of self-worth and affirm his or her own. Ironically, what seemingly affects Dr. English most deeply in Julian's death is Deputy Coroner Moskowitz's satisfaction in recording the death as a suicide—an act of revenge, he is certain, for his failure to have invited "the little kike quack" to the County Medical Society dinner. "Let

Moskowitz have his revenge," he reflects. "Dr. English would have something to say hereafter about the deputy coronerships. Without that Moskowitz could not live." By the end of the novel, a work strewn with the imagery of warfare, Julian English comes to seem like a soldier who has fallen in battle.

 But Julian's problem lies also within himself. Haunted by a sense of inadequacy, he is weak in many ways. His life shows a pattern of drift, of a too-easy accommodation to his immediate environment. His ownership of the auto dealership was made possible by his father's money, not by his own energy and enterprise. The status symbol associations of the Cadillac itself underscore Julian's adoption of outward forms to bolster his life, his failure to earn a meaningful sense of himself. He has bolstered himself with illusions of popularity, position, and sexual adequacy, but once the harsher realities of his life are laid bare to him, he is unequipped to cope with them. He has mismanaged his business, become a debtor to Harry Reilly; his wife rejects him and his best friend turns on him. He takes refuge in drink, his mental processes blur, and as one disastrous occurrence follows another his life becomes intolerable to him. It has been said that O'Hara pushes Julian to his death, but his disintegration is, after all, plausible. It is *just* possible that his debacle at the country club will involve him in a series of other incidents and that, given his personal weaknesses and the impairment of his judgment by alcohol, he will reach a point of ultimate despair. One of the fascinating features of the novel is the way in which pure chance operates through it while at the same time Julian's death seems almost deterministically decreed.

Julian's marriage to Caroline Walker English is especially critical, since what is at issue between them bears on the theme of the novel; the rift between them exposes Julian's inadequacy, the consciousness of which

he has until then been able to repress. She is a reasona-
ble wife for Julian, since she is of good family, a Bryn
Mawr graduate from his own home town. They had
even grown up together. They have, however, quar-
reled enough in the past for other people to be aware
of it, and under stress they are unable to understand
each other. Caroline seems almost to have drifted into
her marriage to Julian. Two other men figure in her
past, and one of them, Ross Campbell, would, but for
an accident of separation, have made the most suitable
husband for her. Later, she is said to have "fallen in
love" with Julian. Her love, however, is not uncondi-
tional. For one thing, their partnership is sexual, and
Caroline is not entirely at ease with sex. There is more
than a hint in the novel that Julian makes sexual demands on her that she cannot entirely respond to. After
the incident at the country club, Julian and Caroline
have sexual relations, and O'Hara comments that it
was the one time "she did not fail him," making the
reader feel that there were other times when she had.
Moreover, this relaxation of tension between them is
only momentary. What the marriage reveals most
deeply is a tremendous uncertainty of communication
between them.

A failure of communication comes to include all
the other characters, and in a sense it is what the novel
is about. O'Hara's handling of this theme is especially
impressive, inasmuch as it is oblique, is never the subject of comment. In certain cases, individuals are characterized entirely through the way they speak. When
Julian and Caroline visit Dr. English and his wife for a
Christmas day cocktail, Dr. English's remarks have a
certain dryness that speaks volumes about his relationship, or lack of it, with his son. Even in the late scene,
after Julian's suicide, when Caroline cries out at him
hysterically that he had never shown his son love, it
can be noticed, through his speech, that Dr. English is

able to maintain his "dignity." Similarly, when Caroline goes to talk to her mother about her unhappiness, which by then has become desperate, Mrs. Walker's speech reveals her as belonging to a serenely sheltered, earlier-day world that has little to do with the realities of the present "Prohibition age." There is even some humor in her assumption that she is an ideal marital confidante for her daughter. O'Hara's characters talk at cross purposes, and there seems no real communication anywhere in the identityless world that O'Hara depicts. It is this sense of unintelligibility in attempted communication, and not Julian's tragedy alone, that contributes to the darkness of the novel's vision.

Appointment in Samarra is often regarded as a naturalistic novel that charts the destruction of its hero through a close notation of his personal weakness and the social forces that act against him. This interpretation of the novel is partly justified, but it does not entirely bring out its special quality. *Appointment in Samarra* is a work of considerable aesthetic intelligence, and a certain kind of irony plays over it, making it seem problematic. One notes at times a peculiar type of humor, peculiar to O'Hara himself, that keeps appearing in it, and suggests a flickering modulation of vision, the difficulty of perceiving reality accurately at all. In commenting on the enigmatic quality of the novel, Lionel Trilling has compared O'Hara to Kafka:

When once we have conceived the idea of general essential humanity, nothing can seem more irrational than the distinctions which people make among themselves. They are absurd, and the society which makes up the sum of the distinctions, and has the duty of controlling them and of adjusting them to each other, shares their absurdity. Like most writers who effectively represent in the full details of its irrational existence, O'Hara is half in love with absurdity. The other half of his feeling is fear. I suppose that there are no two writers who at first glance seem more unlike than O'Hara and Kafka.

Yet there is a recurrent imagination in O'Hara that brings him very close to the author of *The Trial*. It is the imagination of society as some strange sentient organism which acts by laws of its own being which are not to be understood; one does not know what will set into motion its dull, implacable hostility, some small thing, not very wrong, not wrong at all; once it begins to move, no one can stand against it. It is this terrible imagination of society which is the theme of O'Hara's first novel, the remarkable *Appointment in Samarra*.[7]

Socially recognizable as Gibbsville is, there is yet something about the community as O'Hara has represented it that is disturbing, and above all mysterious. The laws of chance that operate in it cannot easily be explained. At least one critic, Arthur Mizener, has argued that O'Hara's depiction of Julian is unacceptable, since it is unclear exactly what impulse within him is responsible for his self-destructive behavior.[8] But this uncertainty about his deepest motivation need not, in this case, be regarded as a flaw of characterization. It is consistent with the pattern of the novel that the sufferer should not himself know why he suffers, that he should lose everything without knowing why.

It is part of the inexplicable in the novel that Julian, on his way down, should keep brushing up against the unexpected or irrational. How improbable it is, for example, that the one character he encounters who understands and even sympathizes with him for having humiliated the Catholic Harry Reilly is Monsignor Creedon. How absurd it is that Julian's best friend, Froggy Ogden, should suddenly reveal the hostility he has always harbored toward him, while Reilly, when he finally speaks, should disclose a genuine affection for Julian. It is unsettlingly bizarre, in the next-to-last episode of the novel, that Ross Campbell, who would have made the most suitable husband for Caroline, and "Polish Mary," who might have been best suited for Julian, should meet and enter into familiarity in the cocktail lounge of another city.

The novel is framed by the Christmas holiday, the time of the birth of Christ, and the promise of a coming together in oneness and love, but what Gibbsville represents, and what broods over it, is a fragmented, lonely unintelligibility. *Appointment in Samarra* is full of interest of a forward-looking kind, since it looks ahead to such later fiction as Styron's *Lie Down in Darkness* (1951), in which the anguish of its characters is underscored by the disintegrative life of the country club, and Cheever's *New Yorker* stories of lonely, bewitched suburbanites. But, most of all, the work's interest is intrinsic, for it shows how masterfully O'Hara could engage his theme of isolation in a complexly organized mosaic novel. In its tautness, suspenseful pace, and bitter but intricate vision, *Appointment in Samarra* is O'Hara's most nearly perfect novel. Few American writers have begun their careers in the novel with such command and distinction.

4

Butterfield 8 and Hope
of Heaven:
Completing the
Trilogy of the Thirties

Butterfield 8 (1935) was published immediately after
Appointment in Samarra and is similar to it in a number
of respects. In both novels, for example, O'Hara
creates a special time and place—Gibbsville and then
New York City in the Prohibition era of the early 1930s.
Butterfield 8 is unusual for O'Hara in its having been
inspired by an actual incident—the death and scandal
surrounding it of a young woman named Starr Faithfull. After the body of Starr Faithfull was washed
ashore on Long Island early in the summer of 1931, an
autopsy revealed that she had been drugged and had
sustained multiple injuries before drowning. The sen-
sational case, with its implications of foul play, was
never solved, but continued to make newspaper head-
lines during the rest of that summer. The twenty-five-
year-old Miss Faithfull lived at a fashionable New York
address but had led anything but a conventionally respectable life. Her drinking, promiscuity, and affairs,
some with socially prominent men in the city, were all
brought out. It was also revealed that as a schoolgirl
she had been debauched by a wealthy, eminent citizen
of Boston, former Mayor Andrew J. Peters. Although
O'Hara did not cover the story for a newspaper, he

had seen Starr Faithfull at speakeasies, had acquainted himself with the case and, for a time, was even in possession of her diaries. In *Butterfield 8*, Starr Faithfull becomes Gloria Wandrous, whose squandered potentiality and brutal death give a unique perspective on her time and place.

Butterfield 8 is like *Appointment in Samarra* in its having the form of a pattern or mosaic novel. It is related in a series of panels, which introduce characters who interact with or have some tangential relationship to one another. The entire novel takes place in less than a week's time, beginning on a Sunday morning in May when Gloria Wandrous awakens alone, in brassiere and panties, in the apartment of a well-to-do man whom she had met only the night before. She covers her near nakedness with a mink coat that belongs to the gentleman's wife, goes out onto the street, and on her way to the Village takes a taxi that nearly strikes a young couple at an intersection. With the effect of a camera cut, the narrative shifts to another young woman, Isabel Stannard, as she awakens, also in brassiere and panties, the same morning. She dresses quickly and greets James Malloy, a young newspaper reporter, when he arrives at the door of her apartment. They go down to the lobby in an elevator with a couple named Farley, and outside are almost struck by a taxi— with a young woman wearing a mink coat seated in the back. The narrative then shifts to the Farleys, revealing their background, especially Nancy Farley's religiously sheltered one; and, with another "camera cut," to an older man carrying a black Gladstone bag who scours the city in search of Gloria.

O'Hara's method in the opening chapter is a model for the chapters that follow, with additional characters introduced in fragmented segments and suspensefully paced transitions to other scenes occurring at the same time or in the course of immediately ongoing time. Often these characters cross one another's paths, and their interrelatedness in a larger or more encompassing action gradually emerges. O'Hara's New York setting and narrative method are similar to the setting and method of Dos Passos's *Manhattan Transfer* (1925); and like Dos Passos, O'Hara uses his fragmented scenes to introduce motifs that help create the time. In a newspaper article, President Coolidge extols an official for representing the strong character and high purposes of a vanishing era, while other articles note the collapsed state of the economy, the arrest of Legs Diamond, and the manhunt on Long Island for another notorious gunman, emphasizing the prevalence of crime and social disorder. The nature of the time is evoked, too, through O'Hara's use of the speakeasy (twenty thousand of them are located in the vicinity of Times Square alone), where many scenes are set and where almost all the characters go to drink.

The speakeasy episodes and other scenes that demonstrate a random meeting of characters with diverse background also reflect O'Hara's concern with social differences. Some of the characters, like the Liggetts and the Farleys, have money and are well placed socially; others, like Malloy and Eddie Brunner, the young cartoonist, come from families that have lost their money and are at the lower edges of respectability; at a lower level still are the uneducated, the dispossessed, the sexually sleazy, and the dangerous. In an early scene, Malloy argues with Isabel Stannard, who has attended Bryn Mawr and has establishment attitudes, over his socially unassimilable "Mick" background; at other points in the work characters see themselves in outsider or outcast roles while others, on the other hand, are painfully constricted by the "proper" roles that their social position requires them to play.

A minor character, the Jewish parvenu Percy Kahan,[1] is revealing in this respect. Kahan, who has made money in Hollywood, has the architect Farley design a large house for him on Long Island that he hopes may be photographed for *Town and Country*. His presence in the novel intimates that a superior social position may be bought, and hence is artificial. Traditional social forms are still observed by members of the upper middle class, but they have become increasingly irrelevant to life in New York as it is actually lived and to the general loosening of morals in the Depression. Many characters are torn between a formal observance of the traditional codes that are vanishing and an involvement in the morally heedless life that surrounds them.

Gloria Wandrous's dual nature is suggested even in her name, which combines the brightness of "wonder" with the paleness of "wanness," of disillusionment. As a girl she had been betrayed by a series of male authority figures. A Major Boam, a house guest, had kissed her provocatively when they were once alone at her house. It was a psychologically disturbing experience, although mild compared to her debauching later by the educator Dr. Joab Reddington. No longer able to trust men, or the received values they represent, she takes up a life of drinking and promiscuity. Yet she is not a young woman who has had all her ideals destroyed so that she can believe in nothing. It is her problem, rather, that she cannot quite believe but also wants to believe. Part of the time she lives, respectably, at the proper home of her mother and bachelor uncle; yet at other times she frequents the city's speakeasies and is a member of its *demimonde*. Whether in one setting or another, she has to close one half of her life out of her mind. The conflict she suffers is apparent as the novel opens and she awakens in Liggett's apartment. She is remorseful, condemning herself as "bad" and "evil." In the dichotomy in Gloria's mind, the institutionally sanctified earlier values are projected as being wholly "good," the sexual life wholly "evil."

What makes Gloria more than the special case she might at first seem is that her conflict is reflected in the society generally. Both Reddington and Liggett, at different times, although they are more than willing to make use of her sexually, think of Gloria as "evil." They believe that she has polluted or contaminated them. Finding, on his return to his apartment, that Gloria has used his toothbrush, Liggett feels repelled and does not want to touch it. Liggett's thinking, like Gloria's, reveals a dichotomy between the institutionally sanctified "respectable" woman and the "evil" sexual woman. A number of wives appear briefly in *Butterfield 8* and reveal a pattern of sheltered upbringings and sexual repression. Eddie Brunner's mother, for example, is kept in ignorance by relatives that her husband died while attending a hotel party of a sexually promiscuous nature. In a well-turned comic passage, O'Hara remarks that "when it came time to acquaint Eddie with the facts of life, and Roy acquainted him with them, his wife said to him: 'How did you tell him?' The reason she asked was that she still had hopes at that time of finding out herself."

Nancy Farley had been brought up in a strict Catholic household, one in which sex education was considered "undesirable, unsanctioned." Even by the time she marries, her mother has told her nothing whatever about the realities of sex and marriage; and when her baby dies at birth she feels the bitterness of a betrayal. In *Appointment in Samarra*, O'Hara notes the confusion created for the young by the reticence and genteel hypocrisies of the older generation in a Prohibition age of raw sexual realities. He even implies that Julian English's sense of virility and self-worth has been damaged by this confusion, and is a factor in his death. In *Butterfield 8*, the conflict between the old values and present realities disturbs Gloria's sense of herself, and leads in time to her death.

Of the wives in *Butterfield 8* with whom Gloria is implicitly contrasted, the most important is Emily Liggett. Emily Liggett comes from an old Boston family, sheltered in its money that had been made in New England cotton mills. What she is like is suggested in an acutely observed scene where she has lunch with her husband at his club. She is said to have the eyes of a woman who might have headaches, and has a habit of watching her hands when she is using them, as if she were "checking up on their efficiency, their neatness." Emily Liggett does not appear extensively in the work, but she is a character drawn with absolute fidelity—felt not only in what she says but also in what she refrains from saying. Her restraint is particularly dramatic in the scene where her husband finally tells her the truth about the missing coat and his involvement with Gloria. Her "dignity" and consciousness of her superiority to her husband reveal that she knows how to deliver a snub. She is, however, not all that she seems. She had slept with Liggett before their marriage, and in his heart he cannot forgive her this lapse, considering what she and her lineage were supposed to represent. Moreover, when she and the children were vacationing on Cape Cod, he had been seduced by her best friend, Martha Harvey, who also has guaranteed New England credentials. Liggett's many affairs thereafter suggest a disillusionment with the sanctities handed down by the older generation, and in this respect Liggett is similar to Gloria, who has been disillusioned by male authority figures.

Liggett's attraction to Gloria has some very peculiar overtones, which force the reader to ask what she represents to him. He is forty-two, and she is twenty years younger—young enough to be his daughter. O'Hara, in fact, points this out expressly. When another character tells Liggett that Gloria could be his daughter, he replies jokingly that he is going to adopt her: "a few papers to sign and she's my daughter." Now Liggett has a daughter of his own, Ruth, who is nearing but is not yet of adult years; he regards her idealistically as immaculately young and pure. When he leaves Gloria asleep in his bed, the first person Liggett encounters in the street is Ruth, and in this way a connection of some kind, not as yet clear, is implied to exist between mistress and daughter.

Even before Gloria meets Liggett, she is depicted as having a kind of Lolita quality, attracting the interest of older men. A sexual attraction to her is hinted at in her bachelor uncle, William Vandamm, who calls her "Baby." She is still a young girl when Major Boam fondles her, and although she is older when she encounters Reddington, she is still not yet of age; and Reddington's history as a molester of pubescent girls makes it clear that he regards her as a child. Even Eddie Brunner, with whom she has a platonic friendship, is tempted by her but considers that were he to yield to his temptation he would be going to bed with his "kid sister." All these associations reinforce the impression that there is something of an unnatural or incestuous nature implied in Liggett's involvement with Gloria.

O'Hara's intention becomes clear only gradually and in the context of the novel's more encompassing motifs, the most conspicuous of which is the disintegration of faith or belief in a corrupt age. The stock-market crash of 1929 and the Great Depression that follows it make the sureties and "truths" of the old order seem like treacherous lies. Men of Liggett's class are forced to examine themselves and their marriages and are no longer sure that they even have wives. The divorce rate in this set soars to something near 100 percent. Beneath the veneer of transmitted respectabilities, the society presented in *Butterfield 8* seems about as bleakly disillusioned and compromised as it could be. If Liggett is no better than he should be, it must be remembered that he belongs peculiarly to his class and moment.

Liggett is a well-connected Yale graduate and yachtsman, but he could not be called a strong figure. Like Julian English, who bought his Cadillac dealership with his father's money, Liggett owes his position to his family. He is the New York branch manager of a heavy-tool manufacturing plant once owned by his grandfather but since acquired by another firm. He is on the board principally because his family name may still attract business; and although he votes family stock, he votes as he is told by the attorney for his father's estate, who is also a director. Acting on his own in 1930, he has lost in the stock market so heavily that he has reduced his income for the year by two-thirds. Such a background suggests a man who, in the rude awakening of the Depression, has had his belief in himself seriously shaken. How could he not know that his life is chiefly veneer, that he is not what he is supposed to be?

Liggett's exposure to the city's speakeasies would itself be a cause for demoralization. Among the background characters at these illicit dives where a law-enforcement officer, "Fat Eddie the cop," goes to drink, are a waiter with a face made lividly scarlet by acne rosacea, and a bartender with a deceptively innocent face resembling that of Babe Ruth. In a passage that may at first seem gratuitously bitter and misanthropic, O'Hara details the types of people who are found at the speakeasies. They include well-to-do women who have lovers and esteemed professional men who go there to meet their women or who are recovering from venereal disease. One woman, the wife of a famous sportsman-financier, had had four miscarriages before being informed by her doctor that a certain infection contracted from her husband was responsible for her misfortunes. Her presence at the speakeasy indicates that she no longer has as many innocent illusions as she once had. It is worth noting, moreover, that she has the venerable name of Lincoln. Lincoln and Babe Ruth, cherished icons of American life, are debased in O'Hara's description of the people at the speakeasies, a description that seems inspired by Fitzgerald's famous list of those who came to Gatsby's parties.

A spoiled idealism also takes the form of continual strife between characters, particularly between men and women. A man and woman are seen quarreling at one of the speakeasies, and Isabel Stannard and Malloy quarrel early in the work when he takes her to a movie, *Public Enemy*, about a cankered corruption within American society, that offends Isabel's "good taste." Later at a speakeasy, they quarrel again, and Malloy leaves abruptly with Isabel, humiliating her in public. In the opening chapter, tempers flare when a cab driver almost strikes Malloy and Isabel at an intersection. Goaded by Gloria in the back seat, the cab driver shouts, "I'll spit in your eye," a threat meant to undercut their dignity, to bring them down to gross realities. All these seemingly unrelated incidents reinforce the implication of the apartment scene where Liggett tears open the front of Gloria's dress, humiliating her, stripping her of any genteel illusions she may still cling to.

In chapter three, as Liggett recalls the scene in his mind, he likes to think of how Gloria looked when he tore her dress and stripped her, her dignity suddenly broken. Then she was "frightened," was "pitiful and sweet." "Pitiful and sweet," helpless and overawed, she becomes a "child." She becomes what Liggett most desperately longs to recover—lost innocence. The problem is that her involvement in the sexual act cancels out her innocence. Reddington is convinced that the seemingly innocent girls he corrupted were more corrupt than he, and his bitterness suggests that of a man betrayed. In a related way, Liggett has a conflicted sense of Gloria, through whom he seeks a recovery of innocence yet must necessarily find this innocence tainted by her sexuality. What Liggett projects upon Gloria could as well be projected upon his daughter Ruth, whose innocence he has idealized and wishes to keep wholly apart from sexual knowledge. Ruth's presence in the work gives an incestuous implication to Liggett's relationship with Gloria; and if not literally, then in type or on a level of metaphor, the relationship could be called incestuous. It encapsulates Gloria within Liggett's own psychological conflict to the point where she is unable to achieve an identity of her own.

If Gloria is still a child, as men in the work respond to her as being, then she cannot be an adult, a wife, a mature member of society. Her taking Mrs. Liggett's mink coat and her reluctance to give it up suggest that she covets a wife's place, a wife's acceptability and assurance of her identity. At the opening she goes out onto the street wearing a brassiere and panties, covered by the mink coat, but with no dress. The missing dress is her missing identity. On the one hand she longs for a stable adult identity, but on the other she is too disillusioned to believe that institutionally sanctified wifehood is other than a falsehood. Her conflict is deepened, moreover, by her acceptance of male sexual projections upon her as a child-woman, which makes her at once too "innocent" and too "evil" to be assimilable into society. Near the end Gloria receives a call at home from an old school friend who has a last name that is the first name of a boy, Ann Paul. Suavely, O'Hara implies a lesbianism in her past by seeming to dismiss it as an unfounded school rumor. But Ann Paul has now become engaged to a medical student and seems headed for a conventional marriage. Gloria finds herself envying Ann Paul and, feeling very disturbed, goes away to think out her problem. By no coincidence surely she dies on board a ship midway between New England and New York, the intermingling of whose cultures has confused her sense of identity.

One of the patterns that can be noticed in *Butterfield 8* is that of characters who touch one another tangentially in their lives but fail to make real contact. Malloy had once met Eddie Brunner and goes to see him at his apartment at the end, but although his path had crossed Gloria's, he had failed to meet her. Reddington searches for Gloria in the city, and takes a taxi to Eddie Brunner's building, where Gloria actually is at the time, but seeing Norma Day go inside, he becomes confused, believes that he must have the wrong address, and has the taxi drive on. O'Hara's use of vehicles in transit (taxis, cars, trains, and ships) and characters' itineraries that intersect without establishing meaningful contact contributes to the sense of uncertain or foiled communication. When Gloria attempts to be something more to Liggett than an illicit child-woman, to be a possible wife, the tensions between them on board the ship lead to her death. She is literally ground to pieces in the revolving engine blades of *The City of Essex*, which might better have been called *The City of Sex*.

Liggett sneaks away from the ship after it returns to New York, clinging to his respectability through the use of the pseudonym Mr. "Little." Later he appears at Eddie Brunner's apartment to obtain the mink coat, which Brunner returns to him with hardly concealed disgust, knowing that Liggett has valued the coat, a token of respectability, above Gloria. Wonderfully placed at the very end of the novel, Reddington is also shown, reading newspapers nervously and practically shaking with fear that he may be implicated in the notoriety surrounding Gloria's horrible death. At the opening, like the carrier of a virus, he had circled ever closer in pursuit of Gloria; at the end he moves even farther back from the wreckage of her life to the respectability of a well-approved hotel in rural New England, where he vacations with his wife and family. Hypocritically, both seem to disclaim any responsibility for Gloria's death, which makes her seem, more than ever, a victim, a character sacrificed by men and, more generally, by her culture.

Although they may not be immediately apparent, a number of similarities can be noted between *Butterfield 8* and Fitzgerald's *The Great Gatsby*. O'Hara's working in of many symbolic details and use of incremental motifs have a far stronger affinity with Fitzgerald than with the proletarian realists of the thirties; indeed, O'Hara's symbolic underplot or symbolic action underlying surface events follows Fitzgerald's method in *The Great Gatsby* very closely. Moreover, both Fitzgerald and O'Hara use their New York settings to evoke an era of confusion and disturbed values in which characters may be maimed or destroyed heedlessly. O'Hara's doomed central figure, who dies in attempting to cross over into respectability, or authenticity, and is then repudiated by characters who reveal the forces that had created this character's inner conflict and undoing, has been anticipated strikingly in Fitzgerald's novel of the 1920s.

A comparison with Fitzgerald's novel, however, also reveals the more nearly "documentary" nature of *Butterfield 8*. The characters in *Butterfield 8* are two-dimensional, and although they serve O'Hara's larger intentions adequately, they do not generally have the crispness or sharpness of the characters in *Appointment in Samarra*. Two characters, Emily Liggett and Dr. Reddington, are exceptions; they are whole and complete and in their limited way have an intensity of effect. Certain other characters, however, like Norma

Day and Isabel Stannard, are introduced merely to further the plot, or to advance the symbolic underplot, and then drop out of the novel when they are no longer needed.

Gloria Wandrous is always believable, and has been grasped fully through her psychological makeup; but she is held at somewhat too great a distance from the reader to permit a deep identification with her. She also has some unclear edges, both when she is at home with her mother and uncle and when she is shown aboard the ship. Her death on the ship seems somewhat too "managed." O'Hara manipulates her on board, and then arranges her fall from the restricted upper deck into the churning mill of the ship's engine works. In other words, a certain stiffness as well as finesse can be noticed in O'Hara's handling of his characters. But on the whole, and despite some limitations, *Butterfield 8* does create its special world of New York in the thirties; one always remembers Gloria Wandrous and what happened to her in the city. The novel is suspensefully paced, and even as it captures social surfaces authentically it also searches beneath surfaces to explore its theme of sexual trauma and cultural disintegration during the thirties.

In *Hope of Heaven* (1938), which follows *Butterfield 8* by several years, O'Hara shifts his setting to Hollywood, and the novel has special interest inasmuch as it launches O'Hara's Hollywood fiction. *Hope of Heaven* grew out of O'Hara's own experience as a screenwriter in Hollywood[2]—an assignment that led to later ones, and to his writing a number of plays as well.[3] Film and theatre people supplied characters for approximately fifty of O'Hara's short stories and several of his novels. The later theatre and Hollywood fiction shows O'Hara refining upon some established themes, but *Hope of Heaven* was written early and is particularly revealing as O'Hara's first attempt to set down and "define" the Hollywood experience—to write a "Hollywood novel."

Hope of Heaven may also be regarded as the final installment of O'Hara's trilogy of novels, begun with *Appointment in Samarra,* portraying American life and disintegrating values in the 1930s. The progression of setting in these novels, from the American town to New York City to Hollywood, reveals an increasing sense of a dissolution of traditional standards, with the effect that, in the final work, such standards seem only a dim memory. O'Hara's characters in *Hope of Heaven* have essentially anonymous existences. Hollywood seems less a city than a population mass, an accident of geography; and the characters who inhabit it have an unclearly defined relationship to one another. One of the most interesting features of the novel is the way in which O'Hara has refrained from describing Hollywood in any detail, so that it seems an almost vacant space traversed by characters in search of their identity.

Hope of Heaven is narrated by James Malloy, who had appeared earlier in a more incidental role in *Butterfield 8* and will appear again in various nouvelles and stories, somewhat like James T. Farrell's recurring character Danny O'Neill.[4] At the time of the novel, Malloy is in his mid-thirties and divorced, and is a sometime writer for Hollywood. He has a more definite personality than he had been given in *Butterfield 8,* has been successful enough to be partly cynical; is a womanizer, a drinker, and—in a rather self-conscious way—a "tough guy." As he is first seen, with his feet up on his desk, estimating to the penny the cost of his expensive tie, shirt, and shoes, he seems improbable; one wonders how such a man would be capable of writing screenplays. On the other hand, his hard-boiled manner is deceptive, partly concealing his vulnerability and suppressed romanticism; and he does, after all, become credible as a guide to Los Angeles and Hollywood.

In *Hope of Heaven*, O'Hara dispenses with the pattern novel method that he had used effectively in *Appointment in Samarra* and *Butterfield 8*. The novel develops instead through a sequence of taut personal encounters between Malloy and a number of other characters, whose lives are eventually shown to be closely interrelated. The movement of the work, at least through its first half or two-thirds, is quite intriguing, since it constantly raises the question of where these knotted encounters will lead. An impression is given that a symbolic action of some kind may underlie the hard surfaces of the novel. O'Hara's characters seem almost dimensionless types in an existential equation, an impression that is heightened when O'Hara introduces the "con man," an archetypal figure who had appeared in the work of such earlier American writers as Melville and Twain.

In an early passage, Malloy talks to one of the minor characters, who tells him of his sense of Los Angeles: "It's in a semi-tropical climate. It has a Spanish name, with religious Roman Catholic connotations. A rather large Mexican population and Oriental. The architecture . . . is Mexican and Spanish and a little Moorish. And yet, Malloy, consider this: the really fantastic thing about it is that it's the crystallization of the ordinary, ordinary cheap American. The people. The politics. The cults. These Iowa people that come here and really assert themselves. They do what they wanted to do in Iowa but couldn't. . . . The crazy clothes they all wanted to wear back in Iowa. . . . Fantastically ordinary, cheap, commonplace." Only a year later, in *The Day of the Locust* (1939), Nathanael West would create this landscape surrealistically, but O'Hara has already evoked its bizarre nature. In this setting, strange in its formlessness yet the essence of vulgar, commonplace America, a con man circulates, pursued by a second con man, invested with the powers of authority. Both are products of ordinary American life; they want to succeed, to fulfill the American dream, and they are not scrupulous as to the means by which they achieve success. What is at issue between them is money.

A typicality in the con men, Don Miller and Philip Henderson, is implied in their backgrounds. Miller, whose real name is Schumacher, is the son of a Lutheran minister in Swedish Haven, a town near Gibbsville; but by the time he comes of age he is lured by the prospect of a bigger future than any that can be contained by a minister's rectory. He goes to Washington, D.C., where he finds $5,000 worth of traveler's checks belonging to a Don Miller; forging his signature, he begins cashing the checks, and drifts westward to Hollywood, where he hopes to become successful in films as "Don Mills." Henderson also comes from a standard middle-class background, his father having been a railroad superintendent of maintenance in New York State. He attends Cornell for a year, where he indulges in some high living, then drops out of college to go out to California to make money in real estate. There he marries a Margaret Keith and with the outbreak of World War I is sent overseas in the army. After he returns he deserts his wife, becomes a drifter involved with a variety of women and a number of desultory schemes, usually dishonest, for making money. The careers of Miller and Henderson demonstrate a breaking away from an earlier, traditional home, and in Henderson's case the breakup of a family.

In *Butterfield 8,* the breakup of the traditional American home is implied in the article Malloy sells to the "Talk of the Town" department of *The New Yorker.* His article describes a colony of people who live aboard houseboats mounted on wooden piles on the New Jersey side of the Hudson, and in the spring have a tug tow them to Rockaway, where they spend the summer. Their mobile houseboat lives are a travesty of the firmly placed American home, and imply its disintegration. In *Hope of Heaven,* attention is called to the home through the house that Peggy Henderson (Philip Henderson's daughter) and her brother Keith share in Los Angeles. What is striking about it is that it is an ersatz home. The father had deserted the family years before, so that it has almost never had any head of household. The Henderson mother, deceased at the time the novel opens, had been the head of the household in a sense, but she was occupied with her career for the most part—and from what is said of her, the career is made to seem dubious. Even while her husband was overseas in the army, she had, in order to make her way, been kept by a well-to-do gentleman in Pasadena. After Philip Henderson had returned, only to desert his family, she borrowed money from the man in Pasadena and became a buyer in a clothing store, eventually becoming successful, "respectable." Both parents suggest the corruption of the home through the power of money and success-seeking in America. The home Peggy and her brother Keith share, as if they were man and wife, is a parodic version of the traditional home, and eventually involves them in a problem of identity.

A problem of identity is intimated in the novel through a number of characters who are uncertain of who or what they are. Peggy Henderson, who enters the work as Malloy's girlfriend, is a Marxist but, as a practicing capitalist, works at a bookstore in affluent Beverly Hills. Her relationship with Malloy, which is off again and on again, gives the impression that they cannot make up their minds about each other. As the novel opens, she is also seeing a young man named Herbert Stern, who talks about art of a high, serious, and "pure" kind, but contemplates writing a novel that will be a big commercial success. More important,

Malloy is himself compromised. He takes an instinctive dislike to Don Miller yet also helps him because Miller, the con man, is a version of himself.

Although they are not specified, Malloy refers to some shady episodes in his past and to the fact that he, like Miller now, had once had to use an assumed identity. He had also, like the writer in Hemingway's story "The Snows of Kilimanjaro," been married to a rich woman. Malloy has received some acclaim as a serious writer, judging from remarks he makes and the appearance of his name in newspaper columns purveying gossip about celebrities, but at present he is a highly paid screenwriter. He has "on-again" periods with Peggy Henderson, and "off-again" episodes when he sleeps with a Los Angeles whore. His associations in Los Angeles even include a man with mob connections who had come to Hollywood as a "technical adviser" for a gangster picture, and gone on to become an actor-writer for the studios, using the pseudonym "Jerry Luck." Jerry Luck is yet another con man in a society whose corruption is pervasive.

Philip Henderson is Peggy's actual father, but has been absent from her life since she was quite small, so that he seems both her father and a total stranger. When he comes to stay at the house she shares with Keith, she begins to feel disturbed and turns to Malloy for reassurance. At this point Malloy has just been hired by a major studio and, celebrating, splurges money on an expensive rented house in Beverly Hills, complete with a Negro couple to take care of it. At this expensive house that seems like a Hollywood set, Malloy makes love to Peggy, and presents her with an engagement ring. The incident, which occurs significantly at Christmas, involves a great deal of drinking; when Malloy brings Peggy back to her house, she passes out, and Malloy is then driven by the Negro houseman Jonas to a round of Hollywood parties. Very soon after this incident, a Christmas idyll but at the same time an episode of alcoholic make-believe, Peggy's father kills her brother Keith, shattering any prospect Malloy and Peggy may have of a stable, "normal" life.

Keith's death is particularly relevant to the "incest" theme of the novel, which has baffled O'Hara's critics. Even as astute a critic as Edmund Wilson has described the novel's "Freudian behavior-pattern" as "unfathomable." The Freudian behavior-pattern can be noted in Peggy's relationship to her father and brother, a relationship that in either case has sexual overtones. Philip Henderson is still handsome in his fifties, has attracted and exploited women all his life, and continues to exert this attraction. Peggy is disturbed by the prospect of sleeping alone in the house with him, when it appears that Keith may be absent, because a parental-sexual confusion exists in her mind. Furthermore, Keith almost hysterically resents the intrusion of Philip Henderson into their lives and is possessive of Peggy, as if he were her lover. The tension between the father and son becomes intolerable when Henderson makes advances to Karen Waner, Peggy's close friend and more vulnerable alter ego. Keith and his father grapple, Henderson's pistol accidentally discharges, and Keith dies.

What O'Hara has in mind in all this is that the Henderson home harbors such a conflict of identity as to become finally incoherent. The incest theme becomes comprehensible if it is read on a symbolic level in connection with the identity conflicts of the Henderson house. Read in this way, Henderson would "corrupt" his daughter by imparting his con man's values, having a veneer of respectability, to her—a perversion of his guardian's role. On the other hand, Keith would distort her identity by his pretense that their lives represent normal, wholesome American reality. Keith glosses over what he does not want to see, is callow, and lacks consciousness. He cannot allow that Henderson is, indeed, their real father, and would shield Peggy from life, having her share his own illusions and limited awareness. Both the father and brother attempt to enclose Peggy within their own deceptive versions of reality, and this threat to her identity is evoked by O'Hara on the level of an incestuous threat.

At the end, Peggy is sobered by the tragedy within her family, and she breaks the engagement with Malloy because, for reasons she cannot articulate fully, he reminds her too much of both her father and her brother. Malloy does, in fact, have something in common with them. Like Henderson, Malloy has apparently respectable credentials but has been corrupted by American "con." Like Keith, he is a perennial college boy who can tell himself that his rented house in Beverly Hills, a scene of alcoholic self-indulgence, is a real home. Disabused of his daydream, estranged from Peggy Henderson, Malloy is like many other O'Hara characters at the end: he is alone. Unfortunately, the mood of alienation at the end develops out of circumstances that are too obviously contrived by O'Hara. The scene in which Henderson shoots Keith is wholly implausible, and nothing that grows out of it can be taken seriously. The novel is also damaged by having Malloy as its central figure, since his melancholy at the end is ultimately self-pitying. It may be true that Malloy "sold out," but on the other hand no one forced him to. The novel's vision of the corruption of the world tends to console Malloy for his own weakness, and for this reason *Hope of Heaven*, despite its hard-boiled manner, is sentimental in a way that *Appointment in Samarra* and *Butterfield 8* are not.

Appointment in Samarra, *Butterfield 8*, and *Hope of Heaven* are achieved at differing levels of realization, but they all help to create the 1930s. They focus upon distinctively American settings and create their social surfaces with a striking sense of authenticity. But they also evoke the moral life of the time—the uncertainties and terrors that lie beneath these surfaces. All three novels are filled with a sense of a hostile environment, in which nothing can be trusted—particularly not the received truths of the earlier generation. Ultimately the trilogy of novels is concerned with an expulsion from innocence, the ordeal of alienation and isolation. These themes distinguish O'Hara as an "angry young man" of the 1930s. What could not be foreseen at the time is that O'Hara would remain "angry" and unreconciled to the "impurity" of life, that his inner conflict reflected in his novels of the thirties would never diminish or be resolved.

5

The Family Saga Novels of the Middle Period:
A Rage to Live,
Ten North Frederick,
and *From the Terrace*

When O'Hara began *A Rage to Live* (1949), he attempted a novel wholly different from any he had written before, a social novel having a vast canvas. He appears, however, to have contemplated such a novel as far back as the 1930s, judging by references in his correspondence with F. Scott Fitzgerald. "I certainly think you should undertake something more ambitious," Fitzgerald wrote to him in 1936. ". . . Invent a system Zolaesque . . . , but buy a file. On the first page of the file put down the outline of a novel of your own times enormous in scale (don't worry, it will contract by itself) and work on the plan for two months. Take the central point of the file as your big climax and follow your plan backward and forward for another three months. Then draw up something as complicated as a continuity for what you have and set yourself a schedule."[1]

More than a decade passed, however, before O'Hara's admiration of two writers revived his ambition to write a "big" social novel. One author was Jules Romains, whom O'Hara, in 1949, called "the greatest novelist living today." A novelist of epic sweep, Romains recorded the life of French society between 1908 and 1933 in his twenty-seven-volume collective work *Men of Good Will*. The other writer was Booth Tarkington, whose depiction in *The Magnificent Ambersons* (1918) of the social hierarchy and mores of a midwestern city, and the deterioration of one of its prominent families, O'Hara sought to emulate—with the difference that his own treatment would violate all Tarkington's taboos. "I decided that I would write this novel," O'Hara said in an interview, "as Tarkington might have written it if this kind of treatment could have been got away with in the time *Ambersons* was written, and if Tarkington had not been so totally unlike me in almost every respect."[2]

The opening "book" of *A Rage to Live*, which occupies two hundred and forty pages, centers upon the town of Fort Penn (based on Harrisburg) and on Grace and Sidney Tate, one of the community's wealthiest and most prominent couples. The "book" begins ceremonially at a Fourth of July festival in 1917, held at the Tate Farm, still known as the Caldwell farm, since it is the family estate of Grace Caldwell Tate. People from all over the state gather on the grounds, and Governor and Mrs. Dunkelberger themselves are present. The social importance of the Tates is indicated at the beginning in Irma Dunkelberger's misgiving that it takes away from the dignity of her husband's office that the Tates are able to treat him respectfully and yet casually.

The yokel quality of the governor and his wife suggests the relatively unsophisticated nature of Fort Penn at the beginning of the novel. Karl Dunkelberger speaks with a Dutchy accent, which adds to his popularity with the festival's predominantly Dutch crowd, many of whom are farmers. His wife Irma is largely unfamiliar with society; she teaches Sunday School, has a license to teach the primary grades, and plays the piano and organ. An amusing moment occurs when she visits a bathroom in the Tate house and is shocked by a drawing on the wall "showing a little French boy doing Number One right at you, and the picture of the French girl, no clothing on at all, and not even her body turned so that you didn't have to see lower down."

Dunkelberger, who owns a number of mills, has become governor largely to please his wife. She went to the right people, and her husband bought his election. That his election was "bought," however, qualifies an impression of complete innocence in Fort Penn in 1917. The rest of Book One confirms that its innocence has already begun to be lost.

The opening scene at the Caldwell farm is followed by a flashback of immense length, which fills in the history of the Caldwell family and Grace's birth, early experiences, and marriage. The section moves back in time to 1883 and then forward in roughly although not strictly chronological order with the effect of a fluid collage. The life of Fort Penn is depicted, interspersed with episodes in Grace's life, sometimes taking the form of excerpts from letters or passages of dialogue, as well as particular incidents and sustained scenes. In this way, what happens to Grace is inextricably related to the growth and development of the community. Of major importance is Grace's marriage to Sidney Tate, a New Yorker who, although inheriting nearly a million dollars, is overshadowed by the wealth and long local lineage of the Caldwells. Another critical event is Grace's affair with Roger Banon, an Irish building contractor from the wrong side of the tracks; an affair that leads, when Sidney learns of it, to the couple's becoming estranged. When the country enters World War I, Sidney applies for a navy commission, partly to remove himself from a marriage that is now largely a formality. At the close of

Book One, Grace and Sidney say good night to each other, and what the reader knows of their marriage at this point makes their presiding over the festival, a coming together in a sense of oneness and harmony, seem like a cruel illusion.

A Rage to Live grows out of *Butterfield 8* and *Hope of Heaven* in at least one respect, in the concern it shows with an expulsion from innocence, represented by the breakup of the American home and family. The importance of the Tate family in Fort Penn makes its breakup all the more revealing, since it reflects in an important way on the community itself. Even before the estrangement of Grace and Sidney, early indications of the disintegration of the Tate home are carefully noted by O'Hara. Grace's brother Brock Caldwell, for example, does not need to work and instead devotes himself to writing a history of the Caldwells, a symptom that the family is drawing inward upon itself, that its energies have begun to stall. Even as early as 1908, some slippage has occurred in the Tate family's position. The Tate money has been invested so conservatively in a period of expansive investment opportunities that the Tates are no longer among the five richest families in Fort Penn, but are now merely among the top ten. As time passes the Tate home becomes increasingly vulnerable.

The house that Miles Brinkerhoff hires Roger Banon to build for him next to the Caldwell farm seems an encroachment upon the Tates since the house, the setting of a bachelor's relaxed sensual pleasure, brings sex to the Tates' doorstep. It is at Brinkerhoff's house that Grace first meets and then has trysts with Roger Banon. Her affair with Banon, who has risen angrily from the working class, is a corruption of the old Caldwell "quality," a loss of virtue. The sense of the Tate house by the end of Book One is that of a divided house, its earlier integrity now having given way to pleasure and worldliness.

In the "books" that follow, Sidney Tate contracts polio and dies, together with the Tates' youngest son Billy. Later, Grace has an affair with Jack Hollister, an editor of the *Sentinel*, owned by the Caldwells, and the affair eventually has serious consequences. In this later section, O'Hara emphasizes that the social structure of Fort Penn has been changing. In the period after World War I, the Schoffstal House, an old landmark hotel owned by the Schoffstal family, even more important financially than the Caldwells, is razed by a developer named Kleinfeld to make way for a modern building. The North Park housing development for the upwardly mobile middle class has also become a factor in the city's life. It is here that Hollister lives with his wife, whose brother-in-law is Charlie Jay, a mayoral candidate. Charlie Jay had been Grace's earliest initiator into sex, but neither then nor later does he belong to the Tates' social class. Employed by the city engineer's office, where he engages inconspicuously in graft, he belongs to a rising class in Fort Penn that resents the dominance of the old families and is now challenging their authority. When her involvement with Hollister leads to an ugly scene in public, Grace knows that the resentment in town against her, a resentment that has been growing for years, will make her life in Fort Penn so difficult as to be almost intolerable.

In the brief, foreshortened "postlude," set in New York in 1947, one sees what has become of Grace Tate in the nearly thirty years that have passed since the scandal. She is shown entertaining at her apartment. Her guests include her brother Brock and his wife Renee, both of whom are now old, ill, and pathetic. Present also are Grace's two adult children. Her son Alfred is a successful lawyer, but is unfaithful to his wife and is an alcoholic. Her daughter Anna has had two marriages, one to a man who is Jewish, and a second to a man who is rabidly anti-Semitic; Anna's son by her first husband goes to a good WASP school, but has a conspicuously Jewish last name. Grace's old friend Connie Schoffstal is now a lesbian—the first of many who are to follow in O'Hara's novels—and moves in a circle of short-haired women who have an interest in the arts. Finally, a phone call reveals that Grace is involved with a Doctor Crocker, an unhappily married man. The sharp focusing of this final scene, in which O'Hara himself offers no direct comment, makes it clear that Grace Tate's former certainty of "place" has now disintegrated.

Once having belonged to an important landed family in her region, she is at the end deracinated. The Caldwell farm, a solid and substantial home, has vanished and been replaced by a Manhattan apartment. Grace's life and those of her brother, children, and friends suggest that they are all adrift, anonymous, and unrelated. The final scene is effective in dramatizing what has become of Grace Tate, but it is also meant to indicate what has become of America. It is important to remember that the opening scene at the Caldwell farm takes place on the Fourth of July, celebrating the founding of the republic. O'Hara begins with land and landed families, both gentry and yeoman, and ends with a scene of urban alienation, and in doing so traces the course of the nation's life.

Although *A Rage to Live* is guided by a serious theme, the novel is seriously flawed in many respects. The sheer size of the volume, for example, invites loose, pedestrian writing. The life of Fort Penn is described at such inordinate length that it wearies the reader, who cannot make out why these minutiae are included or how they are supposed to be relevant. Another problem is characterization, which is almost uniformly two-dimensional. Jack Hollister and Charlie Jay, for example, have no features. Roger Banon, a character of some importance, is more an idea than a rounded character, and he is disposed of in a car crash when he is no longer needed. Grace Tate herself is puzzling, since she is a finely felt feminine presence in the work and yet, in respect to motivation, often has the quality of a dummy. Her sexual experiences with Banon and later with Hollister reveal nothing about her because she does not react to them and does not reflect on them. There are important areas of her nature that O'Hara has not filled in.

Much the best part of *A Rage to Live* is Book One, dealing with the marriage of Grace and Sidney Tate. Although Sidney is not fully individualized, he is more nearly a living character than is Banon, and he suffers believable anguish when, after learning of his wife's infidelity, he feels totally alone. His vulnerability is greater, actually, than Grace's; and one wonders about him—what it is in him exactly that is missing, that makes him unable to stand up to the shattering of his illusion about his wife. When he resorts most unhappily to a prostitute, he gives the impression that he has a horror of sex and is filled with fear. Although Grace is made to suffer, it is Sidney, the masculine character, who suffers more; and his suffering has directly to do with the destruction of his sense of his masculinity. Grace's infidelity exposes his dependency, reducing him to a state of weakness. He is in a sense emasculated and can only die. The novel continues for more than two hundred pages after his death, but the reason these later pages read like aftermath is that Sidney Tate and his relation to Grace are at the center of the novel's intensity. *A Rage to Live*, consequently, seems disjointed, a work containing such obvious flaws that one wonders how O'Hara could not have perceived them.

In the period following *A Rage to Live*, O'Hara published two nouvelles, *The Farmers Hotel* (1951)[3] and *A Family Party* (1956),[4] both of which are set in "the Region" and reveal a concise and fully controlled realism that show O'Hara to better advantage than much of the writing in *A Rage to Live*. O'Hara's next novel, *Ten North Frederick*, is also a distinct improvement, and in its directness and the cleanness of its lines gives the impression that a chastening has occurred since the previous novel. In *Ten North Frederick*, O'Hara returns to Gibbsville, which he had sketched earlier in *Appointment in Samarra*, and to the life of its upper middle class. O'Hara knows exactly how this community is organized socially, and how each of its members relates to all the others. Instead of being described at extraordinary length, like Fort Penn, Gibbsville comes to life through the interpersonal relationships of those who live in it.

Ten North Frederick has also been given the most splendid opening to be found in any of O'Hara's novels. The work begins in 1945 with the funeral of Joseph B. Chapin, one of Gibbsville's most respected lawyers, financially well off and with many connections in the state's Republican party. It is typical of the importance of the occasion that the governor himself is included in the distinguished list of Chapin's honorary pallbearers. A large number of characters call at the Chapin house at Ten North Frederick—Gibbsville's mayor, its most prominent bankers, Mike Slattery, a political kingmaker, such highly placed citizens of the town as Dr. English and Whit Hofman, and Paul Donaldson, an industrialist from Scranton. The scene, a full hundred pages long, introduces the many characters who knew Joe Chapin before the reader yet knows the nature of his life, or the role these characters played in it.

Figuring dramatically in the scene is Chapin's widow Edith, who remains upstairs while the characters assembled below—from the town's dignitaries to the help in the kitchen—all talk about her. In an upstairs room she receives Bob Hooker, a newspaper editor who has eulogized her husband in an editorial. To him she confides that she has always lived for her husband and family, having no outside interests—unlike her late husband, who had "complete confidence in himself." When she goes down to meet the callers, she moves among them expertly, bereaved but forgetting no one's name, managing to acknowledge each member of the large crowd. Off to one side, her daughter speaks of her "playing" the gracious widow, and her comments about her mother, like those of her brother Joby, are sharp and brutal. They even speak of her having "slowly poisoned" their father, of having destroyed him. Teasing questions about Chapin and his marriage are raised through a constantly varied sequence of conversations between characters who are present at or have just returned from attending the funeral. O'Hara's strategy is similar to the one he had used in *Appointment in Samarra* and *Butterfield 8*, in which limited sets of characters appear in alternating panels; but in this case the panels are all part of a lengthy, impressively sustained single "scene."

After this funeral scene, the narrative drops back to Gibbsville in 1909 when Joe Chapin and Edith Stokes were married, and then beyond that to the marriage in 1881 of Chapin's parents. Ben and Charlotte Chapin belong to two of the oldest and wealthiest families in Gibbsville, and to all outward appearances their marriage is all that it should be; but in reality it is loveless and unhappy. After the birth of the son and then of two stillborn children, Charlotte Chapin never again sleeps with her husband, who becomes the loneliest of men, and she transfers her love to her son. A matriarchal woman, she dotes on and overprotects her boy, envisioning an exceptional future for him. As much as possible she arranges his life, providing a "trustworthy companion" for him in Arthur McHenry,

with whom he attends Yale and the University of Pennsylvania law school before they enter into a successful,
conservative legal practice in Gibbsville.

She even, in a sense, selects his wife. She sanctions
his choice of Edith Stokes, at any rate, as she would
not have done had Edith been a different sort of
woman. Edith is of good family, but more importantly
she does not, to Charlotte's perception, have within
her any particular capacity for romantic love. "No girl
with a face as plain as Edith's," Charlotte reflects,
"could inspire a love or even a passion that would
cause a son to reject his mother." Joe Chapin, although
successful as an attorney, suffers an emotional or personal paralysis through his involvement with these two
women—his mother, who damages the inner spring of
his emotional life, and his wife, who destroys it.

After their marriage, Joe and Edith Chapin move
in with the Chapin parents at the matriarchal house at
Ten North Frederick. The Chapin parents die before
long, and the Chapin children are born—Ann and, four
years later, Joe, Jr., or Joby. In 1917, when America
enters World War I, Chapin and Arthur McHenry toss
a coin to see which of them will volunteer for military
service and which remain to look after the affairs of
the law firm. McHenry wins the toss, goes into the
army, eventually returning as a captain, while Chapin
remains in Gibbsville to undergo slow suffocation. As
the novel progresses, two lines of development are followed closely—the alienation of the children from the
house at Ten North Frederick and Chapin's confinement within the house despite his attempt to break out
of it through a career in politics. Chapin's secret aspira-
tion to become president of the United States is so un-
realistic as ultimately to make his life seem pathetic.

Emotionally constrained from his youth by a
watchful and dictatorial mother, he does not have the
"feel" of life in him, is always somewhat too formal,

and does not understand politics from the standpoint of human relations. He offends Mike Slattery, which costs him the Republican nomination for lieutenant governor, a position once held by his grandfather. After this particularly stunning defeat, he retires further into the privacy of the house and the company of a wife who comes to feel even more contempt for him than he does for himself. The children, now young adults, have both been damaged by the constraints imposed by their household, and regard their mother with hardly concealed hostility. In the final section of the novel, Chapin drinks heavily, dying sooner than he need have, of cirrhosis of the liver. He dies, one is made to feel, of loneliness.

In *A Rage to Live*, the dissolution of a family is dramatized by the loss of the home, the sturdily placed Caldwell farm, that had given order, continuity, and coherence to the family's experience. Using a wholly different tactic in *Ten North Frederick*, O'Hara depicts the disintegration of the family *within* the home that remains immovably fixed in place and serves as a constant reminder of the characters' experience in it. The house at Ten North Frederick is the chief framing device of the novel, and gives the work its dramatic focus. It is a family legacy, the house where Ben Chapin had died a lonely and defeated man, and where his son does also. It is the structure from which Joe Chapin cannot escape into "life," very much as the Pyncheon heirs in *The House of the Seven Gables* cannot escape from the confinement of their hereditary dwelling into "the world."

The Chapin house, furthermore, has been given very specific sexual implications. O'Hara points out at the beginning that Frederick Street is no longer the most fashionable address in Gibbsville, having been replaced in importance by Lantenengo Street. Chapin's remaining at the family home puts him somewhat out of the way of the ongoing life of the town; ties him in a tenacious and odd way to the past. More particularly, as a matriarchal house, it ties him to Charlotte Chapin. What is striking about Charlotte Chapin is that she is ill at ease with sexuality. It is repugnant to her, and even before she marries Ben Chapin she plans to have as little to do with it as possible. Her sexual relations with her husband are decidedly short-lived.

It is not so much that she has no sexual nature as that she has suppressed or repudiated it. As a young bride, she walks through a poor section of town to her husband's office and is accosted by a drunken laborer who begins to paw her until Connelly, the Chapins' coachman who has taken the precaution of following her in his rig, knocks the man down with the loaded end of his whip. In taking this unnecessary and unlikely route, she seems to be unconsciously inviting the man to molest her. The impression is reinforced by the fact that she later takes the route again, entirely alone. She suppresses the "beastliness" of her own desires, however; places herself securely above sexuality, limiting and then ending her conjugal relations with her husband. She not only tames her husband but also "breaks" him, punishing him for his sexuality—and her own. Her suppressed sexuality then manifests itself in her devotion to her son, whose manners toward her are said to be "courtly." In submitting to matriarchal domination, Joe Chapin never entirely frees himself from Charlotte, and an evidence of it is that he marries a woman similar to her in the important respect that she, too, is sexually constrained. Edith Chapin is not sexless, but one is always conscious of her sexual distance from her husband. Unable to give herself very fully sexually, she becomes instead Chapin's "manager" and possessor, much like Charlotte.

Somewhat like D. H. Lawrence, O'Hara implies that these women who cannot give of themselves sexually and become perverse "possessors" of men are haters of both sex and life. Although *Ten North Frederick* is elaborately realistic, it does contain passages that are "romantically" heightened in their effect. Charlotte's hatred of her husband is extraordinary in its intensity (it is as if he represents all the sexual release she has forbidden herself); and after his death, when she no longer has anyone to hate, she is depicted as dying of a "poison" that has become blocked up within her system. "It runs through her whole system," one of the Chapin servants remarks, "till her whole system is saturated with it."

Edith's consciousness when she lies in bed at night and thinks of her husband is also projected "romantically," and is even faintly reminiscent of the romantic heightening with which Henry James evokes Isabel Archer's consciousness of Gilbert Osmond ("he put the lights out one by one"), although the context is different:

> But what she owned now was not enough. It was incomplete and he was asleep and distant from her, and the fire they had lit had gone out. And then she began to understand that he was going to take a lot of owning. . . . Now, with his head on her breast, she saw that the desire to own him was not to be so easily satisfied, or possibly ever satisfied. It was not Love; Love might easily have very little to do with it; but it was as strong a desire as Love or Hate and it was going to be her life, the owning of this man. . . . It was going to be as though she had covered him with a sac and as though he depended on her for breath and nourishment. And it was going to take forever. . . . The kind of owning she wanted was continuing and permanent and infinite.

This passage occurs in the same section in which Charlotte is dying from the "poison" in her system, and in this way the futility of the older woman's "owning" passion reflects on the futility of Edith's possessing of Joe Chapin. Charlotte's great plan for her boy's future, which takes the place of sex and love, is duplicated in Edith's great plan for her owning of her husband. Both plans end with a sense of failure and hatred. Everyone within the family is maimed; all are cut off from any nourishing sources of love and suffer estrangement. On one level of its conception, surprisingly, *Ten North Frederick* can be read as an allegory or "morality."

On the level of realism, the novel has a large plausibility. The characters who appear in it tend to be social types, but they are presented knowledgeably; and in Mike Slattery, O'Hara creates a convincing and memorable character. Slattery is wholly dissimilar from Harry Reilly, the crude Irish parvenu in *Appointment in Samarra;* he is a surprising mixture of the shrewd and experienced political manager and the immaculate family man. His wife Peggy is a true partner and a beneficial influence on her husband. The Slatterys have an ease and naturalness in their marital relationship that the Chapins do not. But Edith Chapin is a great presence in the work, and an instance of O'Hara's ability to create women suggestively. The single qualification that might be made of her is that she tends to fade in and out of the novel; and because it is not fully demonstrated, one has to imagine the mechanism by which she has crushed her husband's spirit.

The novel is also less effective than it could be in O'Hara's drawing of the Chapin children, Ann and Joby, whose thwarting experiences as a result of their involvement with the house seem somewhat strained. They are strictly two-dimensional characters, and so, for that matter, is Joe Chapin himself. He is always plausible, but his curious lack of force blocks the reader's identification with him. The too carefully plotted stages of his decline (his fall on the staircase and the drinking that marks the final phase of his deterioration) also make him seem somewhat wooden. Yet despite his inanimate nature, Joe Chapin *does* have a strange hold on the reader's imagination, which derives from his strongly evoked situation—his paralysis and entombment in the family house. Death is the unseen presence that inhabits Ten North Frederick—the setting of Chapin's funeral at the opening and of his death at the end—and makes the work disquieting.

This sense of the imminence of death appears to emerge from O'Hara's own experience at the time the novel was written. In 1953, O'Hara was near death after the rupture of a gastric ulcer, and six months later his second wife, Belle Wylie O'Hara, died of heart disease. O'Hara's marriage to Katharine Bryan occurred in the same year that *Ten North Frederick* was published, restoring some stability to his life but perhaps occasioning other anxieties. The dependency upon women and the threat of emasculation by them in *Ten North Frederick* hint at their having their sources in O'Hara's own inner life. Certain phobic themes in the work, in any case—emasculation by women, paralysis, failure, and death—are felt sharply in the novel, and ultimately give it its life.

In *From the Terrace* (1958), the career of Alfred Eaton is of much larger size than Joe Chapin's, but O'Hara's theme is similar to that in *Ten North Frederick*—the personal failure of a public man. In all three novels of his middle period, in fact, O'Hara reveals common preoccupations: the disintegration of a family, and the failure of a life; and in this respect the three middle novels may be regarded as O'Hara's second novel trilogy. Unlike *A Rage to Live* and *Ten North Frederick*, however, which take place essentially within the confines of certain Pennsylvania towns, *From the Terrace* is national in scope. Although it begins in "the Region," it incorporates many other settings, including New York, the North Shore of Long Island, Wall Street, Washington, D.C., and California, and attempts to document the whole life of America in the first half of the twentieth century.

From the Terrace has the form of a fictional biography of Alfred Eaton; in his opening comments, O'Hara maintains that he is revealing an actual life and that Alfred Eaton is still living. After this opening, the novel proper begins its long journey of nine hundred pages that is uninterrupted by so much as a single chapter division. The unchaptered narrative flow seems a kind of adumbration of the inchoate flow of American experience in the twentieth century. Chronology is handled skillfully by O'Hara, since its forward movement throughout, which might otherwise become monotonous, has been varied at many points. While the narrative moves forward, it also shifts back and forth in time, sometimes through the use of flashbacks, and even of flashbacks within flashbacks. Passages dealing with many aspects of American life are included, and over a hundred characters are introduced. Yet Alfred Eaton is always the central focus of the work, his career running parallel with the developing life of the nation. As an experiment in narrative construction, in a huge work of over half a million words, *From the Terrace* represents a considerable accomplishment.

From the Terrace begins in the Pennsylvania town of Port Johnson, in Lantenengo County, where the Eaton family owns a steel mill. Samuel Eaton, head of the family, is an unsympathetically depicted character obsessed by work, and is implicitly contrasted with his father-in-law Raymond Johnson. From an old, wealthy family after whom the community is named, Johnson is a Bible-reading Presbyterian, and yet is made to seem less rigid than his son-in-law. He is more humanly related to others and has a larger set of values than Samuel Eaton, of whom he has never approved, having found him lacking in "imagination." Samuel

Eaton is so absorbed by the running of his steel mill that the members of his family all suffer markedly. His second son, Raymond Alfred Eaton, suffers certainly, since his father is unable to show him love; he grows up compensating for the absence of love by becoming a high achiever—although at a cost to his emotional life.

The most important lesson Alfred learns as he grows up in the Eaton house is that he is alone. At first through a deprivation of love, and then through habit and preference, in prep school and college, Alfred lives much within himself, becoming independent and competent. But as he attempts to elevate himself in his father's estimation, he misses his "youth." In a sense, he has never been young. When the country enters World War I, Alfred enlists in the navy, but after his discharge at the end of the war, he does not return to finish his degree at Princeton since, although he is only twenty-one, he is now far older emotionally than college students. Nor does he go to work at the Eaton steel mill. The reason he does not, O'Hara remarks, is "that he was not a second-rater. He could have been the leading citizen of Port Johnson without much competition, but it would have been avoiding life and rather cowardly. Port Johnson was not good enough for him. He had to live in the big world, compete with the big people."

Having been left two hundred thousand dollars by his grandfather, Raymond Johnson, Alfred goes to live in New York, where he shares an apartment on Gramercy Park with his wealthy Princeton classmate Alexander ("Lex") Porter. The apartment is the setting of liaisons with young women, but the reader has the sense that these experiences are a temporary phase of Alfred's life, part of his "education" in the world that will teach him to gauge people and their motives accurately. Before long he marries Mary St. John, from a

well-to-do family, and with Lex Porter and his uncles,
the Thornton brothers, founds the Nassau Aeronautical
Corporation on Long Island. While living on Long Island, he meets the influential banker James Mac-
Hardie, and relinquishes his holdings in the airplane
manufacturing venture to go to work for him. As Mac-
Hardie's protégé, in line for a partnership in an im-
mensely important banking firm, he devotes himself to
his work with the force of an obsession. He demon-
strates a mastery of affairs, is trusted, respected, admired; men twice his age consult him. By the time he is
thirty, he becomes a millionaire. In this section, the
novel reads like a romance of money; and at times, in
fact, Alfred makes one think of a more attractive version of Frank Cowperwood, Dreiser's hero of finance
in *The Financier* and *The Titan*.

Later, with the outbreak of World War II, the
scene shifts to Washington, where Alfred becomes assistant secretary of the navy. The corridors of power
are visited; a new cast of federal lawyers, bureaucrats,
and New Deal planners is introduced, and the President of the United States himself becomes a character.
Eventually, Alfred is outmaneuvered by men who
resent his monied origins and integrity. Percy Hasbrouck prevents his succeeding MacHardie at Mac-
Hardie & Company, and even blocks his return to the
firm; and he is placed in the position of seeming to be
compromised in his position with the government. In
California with his second wife Natalie, he suffers a
nearly fatal hemorrhage, and his career ends when he
is only forty-five. The novel concludes in New York,
where Alfred, for whom work has been an obsession,
no longer has anything to do. The solitude bequeathed
to him by his family, although eluded for a time
through work, becomes finally inescapable.

O'Hara later acknowledged that Alfred Eaton was
inspired by an actual public figure, Anthony Eden,[5]

who rose to prominence early in life, became a protégé of Winston Churchill, and was for a time England's prime minister—until the Suez affair terminated his career at the age of fifty-nine. Alfred Eaton's career has a similar pattern of conspicuous early success followed by the abrupt ending of his career while he is still relatively young; but what is more interesting is that O'Hara has given Alfred a psychological history that begins and ends in solitude and resembles his own. Like Alfred, O'Hara had been denied love by his work-driven father, and left his home town in Pennsylvania to compete with the "big people." Alfred had made his first million by the time he was thirty, and O'Hara had published a famous novel at the same age. Alfred suffers a nearly fatal hemorrhage in his mid-forties, as O'Hara had himself. O'Hara's hemorrhage *might* have cut short his career, and had it done so would have made his loneliness intolerable. The case of Anthony Eden appears to have caused O'Hara to reflect on his own life, and to see in Eden's career and what might have been his own a version of "the American loneliness."

Alfred is clearly intended to be representative of American experience. He originates in an American town, located near but smaller than Gibbsville, where the old patriarch, his maternal grandfather Raymond Johnson, reads Scripture on Sunday afternoons in his house called "the Mansion," and has now receded from the center of the town's life. At the center is his son-in-law Samuel Eaton, who conspicuously has no religion, except work and money-making, and deprives his family of a source of love and relationship it must have if it is to survive as a family. His declaring a day off for his workers at the steel mill when his first son is born is an act of pride, separating him from others, since he may if he wishes suspend the usual norms and the regulated life of the community. This act is made to seem like a version of original sin; and is followed before long by the disintegration of his family and of his life's work. As *From the Terrace* proceeds, it comes increasingly to envision an America in which lives are fragmented and unrelated. The unchaptered narrative flow of the novel intimates an unintelligibility in its world, a setting in which individuals are no longer in control of their destinies and must all endure isolation.

The sense of a world fallen into discord and contention is accentuated by the class warfare that appears throughout the work, beginning in the opening section set in Port Johnson, where the Eatons are hated by many of the poor. O'Hara is particularly effective in evoking the conditions of the town's working and poor classes—its families that are forced to break up, their children sent to orphanages, when the head of a household is seriously injured or crippled; its outcasts who live at the edge of town in shacks built of abandoned doors. Later, O'Hara emphasizes the emergence of a "new" class, people who in many cases have come up from abject poverty and bring their old animosities with them. Tom Rothermel has risen from dire poverty in Port Johnson, and his animosity toward Alfred Eaton, even though he has helped him, speaks for others in the work who seem eager to avenge themselves upon the "old" class. Eventually the power-seeking and the opportunistic destroy Alfred's career, and that they do so is a comment on American society. Alfred, after all, combines the best attributes of the old class and the new. He comes from a wealthy background, but has a sense of responsibility that goes with position; at the same time, he is self-made, has succeeded on his own—although always with scruples. That there is no place for an Alfred Eaton in the country's power elite reveals what, in modern times, the country has become.

An allegorical work with a sense of original sin at the core of its vision, *From the Terrace* is O'Hara's most ambitious novel, one that brings out some of his strength but much of his weakness as a novelist. The work contains effective scenes and some good character sketches, but far too many of its characters are faceless two-dimensional figures, and some of them are implausibly motivated. The epic sweep of *From the Terrace* also impels O'Hara toward excessive documentation (statistics on every phase of social and economic life are piled up mercilessly as verisimilitude), and toward characterizations that are Dickensian in their having been conceived through a single trait, usually an unpleasant one. It is extraordinary how many characters in the novel are vicious or morally deformed. Tom Rothermel, a poor boy who becomes a labor agitator, is driven not even by ambition, as O'Hara points out, but by pure vindictiveness. Two other poor boys who rise socially and economically— Larry Von Elm, the aircraft designer, and Jim Roper, doctor to the affluent and decadent—are motivated chiefly by a hatred of their betters. Roper's friend Sage Remington, a rich lesbian with a salon of effete friends, hates Alfred because she cannot condescend to him. Percy Hasbrouck and Creighton Duffy, the New Deal politician, inspired by and even compared to James Farley, hate Alfred because invidiousness is at the core of their natures. At one point in the novel, O'Hara refers to humanity as "the suspicious, the angry, the markedly cruel, the loud, the mean, the dirty," and generally one feels that O'Hara has allowed his nihilism to take over the work. Many of his characters seem to exist largely as expressions of an evil almost metaphysical in nature.

Moreover, the disaster that O'Hara visits upon his characters is out of proportion to anything that might normally be encountered in life. Not merely one but

both of Alfred's early loves meet violent deaths—
Victoria Dockweiler in an auto wreck, and Norma
Budd in a suicide pact with her lover. Alfred's older
brother perishes when he is fourteen; his father drops
dead on Alfred's wedding day; his son Rowland is
killed in a plane crash. His friend Lex Porter is not only
killed in a train wreck, but for good measure is decapi-
tated. The many instances in the novel of characters
who become casualties is intended, in part, to reinforce the plausibility of Alfred's own abortive career.
But nothing whatever can make the ending believable.
How is one to believe that Alfred, who possesses remarkable character and clear-sightedness, as well as
many other exceptional gifts and attainments testify-
ing to his effectiveness in even the most difficult situations, can turn into the listless weakling depicted in the
final pages? It is the failure of the ending particularly
that makes *From the Terrace* seem beyond O'Hara's
powers.

As a novel trilogy, *A Rage to Live, Ten North
Frederick,* and *From the Terrace* belong very much to
their period, the late forties and fifties, when American
social fiction was impelled, on the one hand, toward
the documentary novel of enormous bulk and, on the
other, toward studies of salient individuals who, re-
gardless of the position they have achieved, are powerless to control their destinies or find any measure of
happiness. Ross Lockridge's *Raintree County* (1948), a
twelve-hundred-page novel that documents in vast detail the life of a midwestern town, illustrates the first of
these tendencies. John P. Marquand's novels, about
successful professional men who come to recognize in
middle age the inner emptiness of their lives, illustrate
the second. Although O'Hara is enamored during this
phase of his career with bulk, the large scale of his
novels does not conceal that his theme is still what it
had been earlier—human powerlessness. In this re-

spect, it might be noted that O'Hara's preoccupations now merge with those of other American novelists prominent in the 1950s. O'Hara, James Gould Cozzens, and John P. Marquand all came under attack at this time by liberal critics who objected to their concern with the lives and customs of affluent WASPs and to their characters' powerlessness before their environment. These authors might well be compared, but, of the group, O'Hara's envisioning of failure and stultification seems the most bleak and terrible, the most unrelievedly negative in its view of man and society.

Despite their unevenness, O'Hara's novels of his middle period enlarged his scope as a writer, since they established him as a social chronicler of the American town and his own fictional region which, in his future novels and short stories, he would continue to expand upon. His most creditable novel of the trilogy is *Ten North Frederick*, which has an architecture, dramatic unity, and clarity of focus lacking in the other works. *A Rage to Live* has a strong opening, and *From the Terrace* is an ambitious experiment in narrative form; but these novels come to life only fitfully, and are flawed in many very serious respects. However, all these novels were important to O'Hara, whose confidence in himself as a novelist had been shaken by the failure of *Hope of Heaven*. Even if imperfectly, the family sagas bring O'Hara much more fully into the world, to its center stage. The extraordinary surge of creative energy O'Hara experienced in the 1960s can almost certainly be traced to the new confidence in his powers that came out of his work in the 1950s. In the 1960s, O'Hara would continue to search for his "form" in the novel. As his early period was followed by novels of a quite different kind in his middle period, so would his final phase be different still from the middle one, the family saga yielding to the musing inwardness of the psychological study.

6

~~~~~~

The Later Short Stories:
The Expanded Vision

In 1961 O'Hara published his first volume of new stories since 1947. Entitled *Assembly*, it contained twenty-six stories, most of them written during the previous summer at Quogue. *Assembly* initiates the later phase of O'Hara's career in the short story, a period of great productivity and achievement. O'Hara himself, in his introduction to the volume, has recorded the sense of exhilaration he experienced in returning to write short stories after a long absence from the form. "It was the most joyful writing I have ever done," he remarked. "The pleasure was in finding that after eleven years of not writing short stories, I could begin again and do it better; and the joy was in discovering that at fifty-five . . . I had an apparently inexhaustible urge to express an unlimited supply of short story ideas."

The stories in *Assembly* are noticeably longer than the early ones, with two of them, "Mrs. Stratton of Oak Knoll" and "A Case History," nearly the length of nouvelles. The pace of the stories is also more leisurely, revealing an interest in the finely observed textures of social experience. Some of the tales have a sinuous movement and edge their way with an inviting indirectness toward their denouement. The narrator's voice often suggests urbanity—a large acquaintance with the world and the nuances of human behavior. The stories are of widely varied kinds. James Malloy is reintroduced, having grown more suave in the course of time, and in several stories the reader is taken back to Gibbsville after World War I. Aging actors and actresses appear in sophisticated settings, and hard-boiled characters meet in pool halls and bars. A number of the tales are set in the suburbs of New York, and often have a married couple as their principal characters. Characteristically, these suburban couples are fairly affluent and older than O'Hara's early short story protagonists. They have good manners and vote the Republican ticket. Aging is a prominent theme in the tales; some of them, like "The Trip," are shadowed with a consciousness of approaching death.

"The Pioneer Hep-Cat" is one of the volume's more lacerating stories, but in many respects it reads like one of O'Hara's early pieces, since it is told in monologue form by a local newspaper editor as he speaks to an audience of high school students in a small Pennsylvania town. He would like to tell them about a General Corrigan who was born in the town, but he has been told that they want to hear about a Jazz Age musician named Reds Watson, who grew up there. Reluctantly, with obvious discomfiture, he informs them of Reds's life—a case of "great talent wasted." It is somewhat improbable that he would allow himself to go into the unpleasant story before the students, but allowing that he does, the tale gains by being related by such a man as the narrator. The old-fashioned normative and local values that O'Hara has insinuated into his voice authenticate that Reds's life belongs to actual fact, has not been "made up."

At the age of thirteen, according to the editor's account, Reds had one of his arms amputated. As a child amputee, he had a paper route and delivered papers to the town's various saloons, where the patrons insisted that he sing—and drink with them. He drank to take his mind off the pain in his arm stump, and by the time he was twenty, he drank heavily. His face purpled from drink, he became sullen, bitter, and hostile. When not performing as a singer with touring dance bands, he dosed himself with alcohol. Eventually he lost his jobs with the bands, and every remnant of respectability. At the age of twenty-five he was found dead on the band-stand of the Alhambra dance hall in Scranton. The dance hall had been closed for the summer, and as the narrator remarks in the last sentence, "the watchman had no idea what Reds had gone there for."

This great, understated last line evokes a whole world of maiming and isolation. Although Reds's life is an extreme case, one is swayed to give it credence by the reliability of the narrator, who also serves to create internal tensions within the story. He is frankly embarrassed by the account he relates, and seems to discourage the idea that Reds's life was at all represen-tative of the town. He had wished to speak of General Corrigan, a better reflection of community values. In other words, he attempts to cover up, but in the course of the story is forced to reveal a buried truth of the life of the community—the horrible maiming and aliena-tion that existed within its normality.

"The Sharks" is perhaps more characteristic of the volume in its concern with the manners of older, afflu-ent characters. In "The Sharks," the Dennings are cu-rious about a stranger who, at the beginning of the summer, acquires a house in their coastal community. He is an older, well-to-do homosexual, and the Den-nings fear that he may attract a colony of homosexuals and that the old-fashioned nature of the place will change. Later in the summer, they learn that the man has just been murdered by a young gas-station atten-dant he had brought home with him one night. But the Dennings' anxieties are not allayed, for soon, like "sharks," other men of the same background, attracted with an almost dreamlike perversity to the notoriety of the incident, come looking for houses too. The seemingly "safe" world of the Dennings is broken in upon by the strangeness of the world without.

"Sterling Silver," one of the collection's best stories, deals with a middle-aged couple who stay at a fashionable California watering place. Their neighbors in Cabaña 18 are Norman and Irma Borse, a nouveau riche couple who have arrived from Los Angeles in their Rolls-Royce. They are inevitably brought into contact with the Borses, and on several afternoons the narrator and Norman Borse are golf partners. Borse is a developer in Santa Ana, his wife, the former Irma Hopwood, was the "beret girl" pictured on the cover of *Life* magazine and on countless highway billboards across the country as part of an advertising promotion for a product. Her modeling career now over, Irma Dennings' anxieties are not allayed, for soon, like been a factor in the success of their marriage.

One of the striking features of the story is the manner of Borse's speech, which O'Hara has rendered vividly:

"It's an advantage when the wife has money of her own," he said. "I got one of my brothers that everybody knows the only reason why his wife is sticking to him is the money. We weren't always millionaires, the Borse brothers. Al married very young and she'd of been all right for like if he'd of stayed where he was, making a nice living but never very big. He had a used-car lot on Cahuenga, and a nice home in the Brentwood section. But he came in with my older brother and I and inside of three years if you wanted to find her she'd be in Bullock's-Wilshire or I. Magnin's, spending. Which was all right, understand. A man makes a lot of money, his wife is entitled. But she got so she hated him. The more he made, the more he gave her, the more she hated him."

Soon afterward, however, the narrator's wife tells him that Irma Borse sleeps with waiters while her husband is playing golf, is "a sterling silver bitch" he "stole from a billboard" and has to live up to. Everything now falls into place with an expertness that distinguishes the whole narration.

In two other deftly handled stories—"The Girl from California" and "Mary and Norma"—O'Hara varies the setting and social level of his characters. In "The Girl from California," Vincent Merino and his wife, the movie actress Barbara Wade, are in New York from the West Coast. While they are staying in the city they go over to Trenton in a chauffeur-driven limousine to see the Merino parents. The old Italian neighborhood is revisited, complete with the appearance there of State Senator Appolino, who would like to exploit the occasion of their visit politically by having some of his constituents come to meet them. Inside the family house, Merino's middle-aged father speaks of his hernia and of his having been "operated," and advises his son, if he wants his marriage to succeed, to "start a baby right away." His own marriage, however, has sagged into futility and boredom. Vincent and Barbara have dinner at the house, but find themselves feeling uncomfortable and out of place. On the way back to New York, after leaving early, they realize that the family has hated them for their success, mobility, and freedom.

The failure of families also enters into "Mary and Norma," a story about two sisters-in-law. At the end of the story, they talk together in Norma's house, and it comes out that they are both cheating on their husbands, for whom they have no respect or love, and from whom they have received none. Scrupulously observed, vulgar and powerful, "Mary and Norma" is a controlled study in disintegrating relationships that, at the end of the piece, uses the house, stark and bare on the eve of moving, in a suggestive, quasi-symbolic way, just as the

Italian house in "The Girl from California" has also been used to provide a focus for the failure of the familial bond.

In other stories O'Hara plays variations on the theme of aging. "Reassurance" examines the lives of an older couple, the Rainsfords, now retired in Virginia and living away from their former friends in New York. When they are visited by a couple they have known for years, Mary and Henry Roberts, they talk chiefly about friends of their own age, a number of whom have died. After the couple leave, Henry Roberts has a heart attack at the wheel of his car, and the Rainsfords are summoned to join Mary Roberts at the hospital. When they return home, after Henry Roberts's death, they settle back into the little comforts of their life, the little reassurances that everything is normal—while they try not to ask themselves how much time they may have left. The emphasis of this understated tale is on the consciousness of the aging characters, as it is in another story, "The Trip." In "The Trip," an older man plans a journey to London, and has begun to look forward to it. But when friends at his club begin dying suddenly of heart attacks, one in a taxi on his way to the club, he decides to cancel his vacation. His vision of his dying alone in a taxi in a far-off city where no one knows him becomes fixed in his mind, and after the story ends it lingers in the reader's mind as well.

Assembly, with its medley of voices and finely attuned moods, was followed annually for the next several years by a new story collection. The Cape Cod Lighter (1962), published the next year, does not contain as many memorable stories as does Assembly, but was O'Hara's most popular short story collection and attracted a new audience for his short fiction. The title of the volume (some people bought the book, it was said, to find out what the title meant) refers to a device for starting fires in fireplaces, and hints at human fires ignited by an outside agency. But, in fact, the tales contain no extraordinary conflagrations. They are on the whole rather quiet, understated rather than over-stated. A number of the tales have a sketchiness about them, as if O'Hara were content to create an atmo-sphere, a situation, and allow the reader to imagine the rest. In certain cases, however, as in "The Bucket of Blood," these stories that read like sketches are actu-ally carefully worked out conceptions.

"The Bucket of Blood," set back in time in Gibbs-ville, recounts the appearance in the town of Jay Det-weiler, and his rise from transient to elevator operator to manager of a pool hall to owner of a saloon known as the Bucket of Blood. Nothing of a startling nature happens to Jay, but in the course of the story one comes to see his life—the shady policemen whose good will he has had to "buy," the whorehouses located within the same two-block area as his saloon, the thin line be-tween financial security, even if of a rough and dubious kind, and the underworld of the dispossessed. The story has a downbeat ending, and seems to have no great point. Against certain odds, Jay Detweiler has managed to become the owner of a saloon.

"The Bucket of Blood," in other words, reads very much like a vignette. One of the finest features of the tale is simply the richness of its texture, the low-life world O'Hara creates that is absolutely convincing and real. But it is also a story that requires the reader to do some of the work of "imagining," and the hand of the craftsman can be noted in it. O'Hara's description of Jay when he arrives in Gibbsville in his mid-thirties is so brief that it might be overlooked, but it is revealing. He remarks that "already the upper half of his thin little face was shaded blue and his eyes were teary." The de-scription makes him seem unwholesomely starved and desolate. What is striking about him at the end, after having accommodated his sexual needs with prosti-

tutes, and with one in particular, is that he is still unmarried, and most of all, is singularly alone.

The reader's sense of Jay at the end is affected, too,
by the time frame that O'Hara has used. The tale opens
in the past, but at a "present" point in the past, and then
sweeps back to an earlier time and forward again toward the opening. The opening description of the
Bucket of Blood may be almost forgotten at the end,
but it is relevant. O'Hara remarks, in this opening, that
"Jay had an alarm clock on the back bar and on the
wall a large Pennsylvania Railroad calendar, showing a
passenger train coming out of the Horseshoe Curve.
Otherwise the saloon was devoid of decoration." This is
Jay's life—stark, ugly, devoid of anything that might
enhance it humanly, stripped down to clocks and cal-
endars that mark the passing of time before Jay dies
alone and enters the grave.

Two other effectively rendered stories concerned
with characters who do not belong to polite society are
"The Sun-Dodgers," a raw, suspenseful, and ultimately
humorous tale about Broadway "night people" of the
thirties—journalists, bookmakers, and mobsters who
gather in speakeasies; and "The Butterfly," about a
young woman who, to the dismay of her half-respect-
able mother, goes off with a not-at-all respectable
steeplejack. Yet O'Hara is able to move with ease from
one social level to another. "Sunday Morning" takes
place essentially within the mind of a solidly middle-
class suburban housewife, Marge Fairbanks. As the
story opens she has lingered over coffee and cigarettes
in town on a Sunday morning, before driving back
home; but en route her car stalls, and she is enclosed
again within her thoughts. What she thinks is that she
does not really want to return home. The children are up
by now and messing about, and her husband of twelve
years is sleeping with his arms around a pillow. Suddenly she asks herself a question: Who is she? Why is

she living? O'Hara steals into this woman's consciousness as if it were his own; and the same stealthy prob-
ing of women's minds is witnessed in two other tales,
"The Women of Madison Avenue" and "The Nothing
Machine." In these stories O'Hara "impersonates"
women, enters into their intimate thoughts and inmost
natures as only another woman, seemingly, would be
able to do.

At the same time O'Hara begins to make explora-
tory probes of homosexuality. "Jurge Dulrumple," set
in Gibbsville during an earlier time, concerns two
women, Miss Ivy Heinz and Miss Muriel Hamilton,
who as the account opens sing "two-part harmony"
while they travel along a road in a motor car. They
laugh as they recall their earlier experience with
George Dalrymple ("Jurge Dulrumple," jestfully, to
them), a serious, sheltered young bank clerk who is
inept with women, and had proposed to both of them
within a month's time. The word "lesbian" is never
used in the story, but the obvious lack of interest in
men of one of them, and their close association like
that of a married couple, intimate a lesbianism that
makes the courtship of both by the sexually inexper-
ienced Dalrymple doubly amusing.

Another tale with a homosexual implication is "Pat
Collins," a long story that begins in the present and
moves back into the past. The device O'Hara uses in
the story is the same one that he used in *Ten North
Frederick,* in which an opening situation is presented
before the narrative drops back into the past to bring
out its significance. The situation at the opening of "Pat
Collins" is that two men, Whit Hofman and Pat Collins,
once close friends, now merely nod and pass on when
they encounter each other on the street. When O'Hara
reverts to the past of the late 1920s, it is brought out that
Hofman, a social leader of Gibbsville, had befriended
Collins when he opened his new garage and helped to

have him admitted to the Lantenengo Country Club. This act, which ought to have brought them even closer together, has the reverse effect. On their first night at the country club, Collins's wife Madge drinks too much, embarrassing her husband before his friend and his wife. Moreover, almost on sight, Kitty Hofman takes a deep and lasting dislike to Madge, and from that point onward the men are divided by the antagonism that exists between their wives.

As the story proceeds, Pat Collins's situation becomes increasingly painful. To put it very simply, Madge Collins is a woman who has designs on her husband's friend. Kitty Hofman is aware of it, and the complication produces difficulties in the Hofman marriage. They take a world cruise, but instead of mending their differences it merely divides the Hofmans further. Kitty has an affair abroad, and after their return to Gibbsville their marriage is never again very sound. Whit Hofman, emotionally estranged from his wife, has an affair with Madge Collins, and Pat is cut off from the man toward whom he has felt a kind of love.

Although muted, it seems a kind of love. Even Madge, reflecting on Pat's feeling for Whit, asks herself: "did he not all but love Whit too?" Madge has sexual relations with her husband and also with Whit, giving them an odd kind of intimacy, although a very wounding one for Pat. He soon begins to drink at Dick Boylan's speakeasy, and allows his business to go to pieces; and when Boylan observes Pat's troubled state of mind he concludes that it must have to do with either money or a woman. O'Hara comments that it "never occurred to Dick Boylan—or, for that matter, to Pat Collins—that Pat's problem was the loss of a friend." Skillfully insinuated, this undercurrent in Pat's feeling for Whit affects the reader's sense of him at the end. By then, Pat seems bereft of close human ties of any kind. He spends most of his time at his garage, which is open twenty-four hours a day; he is cut off emotionally from his wife and he has no male companions. Each time he passes Whit on the street it is a mocking reminder of the scarring deprivations Pat has suffered.

Unlike *The Cape Cod Lighter,* with its many themes, *The Hat on the Bed* (1963) concentrates upon a single one, that of aging. The manner of the stories, however, is often light, even at times wryly amused. A good example would be "The Glendale People," about an aging film actor who lives alone in a Florida cottage overlooking the Gulf of Mexico, with his souvenirs and framed photographs of movie actors and actresses. He is at first said to be a bachelor, but it later comes out that he is the veteran of five unsuccessful marriages. He is attempting to adjust to associating with rather dowdy, older couples whose circumstances, like his own, are a little pinched, and whom, in his earlier Hollywood days, he avoided and referred to as "Glendale people." Near the end, the New York publisher Carson Burroughs visits him, asking how he is progressing with his memoirs, for which he has given him an advance. At the end it comes out that the poor man, after five years of sharpening pencils and sitting down to write, still cannot begin to put his life down on paper. Comically, he is revealed as a man who, at every stage of his career, has been at sea.

"Agatha" is a gemlike story about a fairly well-to-do older woman who has had three husbands and now lives in an apartment building in New York, where she has a maid whom she shares with another East Side family. Her name, revealingly, is Mrs. Child. Mrs. Child is a trifle lightheaded or absent-minded, and she has in the past had some incidents in which a cigarette left carelessly burning had started a small fire. She knows that she should be more careful, and could even be asked to leave her building as an undesirable tenant. In fact, as the story opens, she has just burned a small hole in the carpet with a cigarette, and is trying to cover it up so that the maid will not know. When the maid appears, Mrs. Child explains hastily that one of her dogs has chewed a hole in the carpet, and that she must have the carpet man come by the next day to look at it. Flushed, she then tells the maid that she will be going out to buy another coat. "Do you think I'm mad, Mary?" she says suddenly, in a remarkable last line. "I *am* a little mad, aren't I?"

Many of the stories in *The Hat on the Bed* are filled with fine "effects," and some conclude with one. "The Windowpane Check" seems close to perfection in its plotting and in the sheerness of its ending. One day on a train an older man notices another man wearing a jacket that seems identical to the one, specially made for him by a Scottish tailor, that he had given to a church auction after his wife's death. As they talk, he learns that it *is* the same jacket, and that he and the other man have much in common as widowers who have tried to divest themselves of painful reminders of their happier pasts. At the end, they become one, in their bereavement and barrenness of their present lives. The elegant craftsmanship of "The Glendale People," "Agatha," and "The Windowpane Check" is also seen in other tales in the volume—in "The Manager" (a collector's item among O'Hara's stories), and "The Man on the Tractor." In "The Man on the Tractor," the Denisons, Pam and George, once, according to Gibbsville legend, thought to have inspired characters in F. Scott Fitzgerald, return to the town later in life, sobered and chastened, to find their romantic past vanished and their contemporaries dead or dying. The story is strongly reminiscent of Fitzgerald's "Babylon Revisited." However, it is not Paris, but Gibbsville— now losing population and its large estates reduced to small parcels of land—that is the scene of the Denisons' reckoning.

The theme of time and aging that is prominent in *The Hat on the Bed* recedes, however, in the volume of short stories *The Horse Knows the Way* (1964), which was published just before *The Lockwood Concern* and reflects at least one of its concerns—that of the character who is cut off from others. O'Hara's orchestration of this theme is accomplished in many different ways, sometimes through characters who suffer a grotesque isolation, or are involved in actual violence. In "The Madeline Wherry Case," a woman driven to the breaking point shoots her husband; and in "The Jet Set," another woman, corrupted by her involvement with a set of sophisticated people, leaps to her death. In other stories, such as "The Bonfire" and "Can I Stay Here?," the isolation theme is treated without recourse to outward violence. In "The Bonfire," a recent widow, a young mother whose husband has committed suicide as the story opens, approaches a group of friends who are having a beach picnic by a bonfire, only to run from the bonfire, suddenly stricken with the sense that she no longer has any "place." "Can I Stay Here?" deals with a teen-aged girl belonging to a well-to-do East Side family, who has become disoriented. O'Hara shifts at the end of the story to the consciousness of the girl, a postponed revelation that has the effect of unsettling eeriness.

O'Hara varies his theme by focusing upon characters who belong to different social strata, and is often most successful in stories whose characters are below the level of respectability. "I Spend My Days in Longing" deals with a transient musician who has fallen into a state of malaise, and eventually commits suicide. "The Law Breaker," one of the best stories, is about a young man of good family who becomes a rum runner in the coastal waters of Florida. The story has an episodic movement, and is notable for its raw atmosphere and tough-guy characters. The slowly gathering implications of the story come together only at the end, when various narrative patterns converge—the protagonist's exclusion first by his parents, then by his lady friend, and finally by the mob.

The writing of *The Lockwood Concern* appears to have energized O'Hara's imagination, for the story collection that follows it, *Waiting for Winter* (1966), is one of his finest and most versatile. In *The Hat on the Bed* and *The Horse Knows the Way*, a dominant theme emerges, but in *Waiting for Winter* many strong themes compete for attention. Not only some but most of the stories in the volume represent O'Hara at his best, and they are of very diverse kinds, taking place in both the past and present and on all levels of society. In these tales, O'Hara uses different types of narration, including the "life chronicle" in capsule, returns to explore Hollywood with greater compassion than before, and brings the formerly marginal figure of the homosexual into closer relation to the mainstream of human experience.

A number of the tales in *Waiting for Winter* are set in Gibbsville at the end of the 1920s. In "Yostie," a widower past middle age operates a bathhouse and refreshment stand at a boating place not far from Gibbsville. To this place comes a sinister stranger who calls himself Mr. Smith. "Smith" is the kind of figure O'Hara does to perfection. He is somehow "dangerous," and has about him a kind of leering sexuality. Yostie, the refreshment stand proprietor, is repelled and yet almost hypnotized by this drifter. By the time he breaks free of him and Smith leaves, however, Yostie has been awakened to the sexual desire he has suppressed, and begins to think of marrying Mildred the waitress by the summer's end. The workmanship of the story is more sophisticated than it might seem. The setting of the story, for example, at a distance from the community but connected to it tenuously by a trolley line, has been used by O'Hara to emphasize Yostie's situation. His encounter with Smith, moreover, reveals a mythic pattern in the tale—a Jungian descent into the unconscious, confrontation with an "outlaw" self, and reintegration of personality.

In each of his Gibbsville stories, O'Hara employs a different method or narrative strategy. In "The Skeletons," he uses an omniscient narrator; but in "Fatima and Kisses," the story is told in the first person by James Malloy, whose point of view is restricted. Malloy, then working as a cub reporter for a Gibbsville newspaper after the death of his doctor father, enters only marginally into the action—although far enough to bring him face to face with a brutal tragedy within a family. The story has the disturbing power of déclassé realism, and it might be inferred that such harsh realism is O'Hara's real form. Yet in another fine tale, "Afternoon Waltz," O'Hara deals with upper middle class Lantenengo Street lives in a way that involves an element of delicate fantasy. "Afternoon Waltz" is about a young man who has been settled with an inheritance but goes blind; in the course of the story of an older woman, a widow who lives next door, teaches him to dance, and they thereafter have an affair. The music of a Victrola waltz can be heard from her living room window at the end, as deprivation and pleasure mingle—with a strangely evocative effect that lingers in the reader's imagination.

Other stories in *Waiting for Winter,* forming a group by themselves, are concerned with Hollywood, but they are rather different from O'Hara's early Hollywood stories. For one thing, their pace is more leisurely, with two of them—"James Francis and the Star" and "Natica Jackson"—the length of nouvelles. For another, O'Hara's hostility toward show business people in the early stories has given way to a more complicated or problematic attitude. While the characters are still limited in various ways, they are now capable of a fuller range of emotions.

"The Way to Majorca" is a comic tale about an actress, Sally Standish, who appears in commercially successful Grade B movies. Before long, however, she will be too old for such roles, and has become concerned about her future. In this, she is similar to Meredith Manners, who has written a number of her films and now plans a retirement in Majorca, where he can live inexpensively on what he has been able to save. Together, pooling their savings, they could live in Majorca very comfortably. Meredith Manners is a man in his forties who, because he has fallen arches, moves very slowly; he dresses in tweeds, smokes a pipe, and is a homosexual. Their elopement makes the Los Angeles papers, which print an account of Sally Standish's former romantic attachments and describe Manners sardonically as "a confirmed bachelor." Side by side with a photographic layout of stills from Sally's films, they print a group photograph of Manners with his friends, who include a hair stylist and an elderly tennis player.

The studio head, the delightful Sol Hamper, is shaken by the marriage and by Sally's breaking her contract with the studio. Yet in the end their marriage and retirement to Majorca, where they will join a colony of Meredith's friends, seems no more odd or grotesque than the film world they are anxious to leave. Even Sol Hamper, admitting that he, too, would like to get out of show business, asks about Majorca as a retirement place. "How are they toward Jews, do you happen to know?" he asks. One of the fine things about the story is the generous quality of its satire. Sally Standish and Meredith Manners are treated humorously, of course, but their working out an improbable *modus vivendi* for their lives is made to seem understandable, and they are even accorded a certain respect.

Sol Hamper, who enlivens the story toward the end, also shows O'Hara imagining new character types in the later stories and expanding upon them. "The Portly Gentleman," another Hollywood story having an element of grotesqueness, deals principally with a stout actor named Don Tally, but the character who is captured best is his agent Miles Mosk. Midway through the story he points out to Tally that he is not dependent upon him for a livelihood, having already provided well for himself and Mrs. Mosk, who owns a "mutation" mink. O'Hara is particularly effective in rendering Mosk's strange speech:

Mr. Don Tally, I got a nice home in Great Neck, a boy serving his internship at Mount Sinai Hospital, another boy studding law his second year at Columbia Law School. And I got annuities besides, to take care of Mrs. Mosk and I the rest of our natural lives. This I got from my ten percent of you and many's another talented artist I kept working steady. A person willing to work steady, I had the experience and the know-how and the numerous personal contacts whereby I pick up the long distance telephone and inside of three–four minutes I got a deal.

In "Natica Jackson," the Sol Hamper–Miles Mosk figure appears as the agent Morris King who, in this case, has brought his wife Ernestine into the business with him. Morris and Ernestine are brought to life immediately through their speech, which comments fully on the nature of their experience in Hollywood, which has hardened them without depriving them of their humanity.

"Natica Jackson," a long story, does many things at once. It creates the studio world of Hollywood, and it examines the thin line separating this professional world of illusion-making and the real world without. In this tale it is, again, or at least partly, grotesqueness that fascinates O'Hara. The story begins with a small whim that makes the actress Natica Jackson take a slightly different route home from the studio. Her turning down an unfamiliar street results in a minor auto mishap and in Natica's finding a lover, a married man with a conventional middle-class background. Yet by the end the most unforeseeable consequences ensue, for the man's "normal" background is not all that it seems. His wife is quite mad (in a startling passage O'Hara actually looks into the madness of her mind), and with a Medea-like vengeance upon her husband and his lover, whose identity she does not know, she drowns her two small children. Strangely, irrationality breaks out not in the illusion industry but in the colorless, repressed world of the middle class. But what is most notable of all in the story is that Natica Jackson, the actress, is treated not as a type, or even more particularly as a Hollywood type, but as a fully dimensional woman.

"James Francis and the Star," a companion story, works with a large span of time, and illustrates the new method O'Hara sometimes employs in the later period. Rather than focusing upon a decisive moment in a character's life, he looks for a pattern in a lifetime's experience—as Fitzgerald had done in his story "The Rich Boy." The story treats the lives of two characters— James Francis Hatter, a Hollywood writer, and Rod Fulton, his actor friend. The vicissitudes of their careers and personal relationship are brought out— their periods of obscurity and success, Fulton's wives (one of whom is shared by James Hatter), the scandal that affects them both, their partial reconciliation later in their lives.

At the end, a question is raised that was broached at the beginning: To what extend has the bond between them had a homosexual basis? Even they are unsure, although the womanizing but still unmarried James Hatter is willing to concede that there may al-

ways have been some on his part. The story unfolds
through ever more elaborate turns of plot, but what is
ultimately of interest is the relationship of the two
male friends. The story suggests throughout a fluid
sexuality, in which there may be crossings over from
heterosexuality into homosexuality—as in the case of
two female characters in the tale. And although James
Hatter and Rod Fulton have no sexual contact, their
sharing of the same woman, and the shifting dominator-
and-dominated tensions between them do suggest a
sexual undercurrent in their friendship. On the other
hand, the story is not merely about their problematic
bonding; in a larger sense, it is about the lack of real
fulfillment in the lives of even the most outwardly successful. Both Rod Fulton and James Hatter have had
some success, and Fulton has had a good deal of it. But
the truth of their lives is that they have both suffered
disappointment, are not particularly happy, and give
the sense of being essentially alone at the end. The undercurrent of sexual attraction between them emphasizes a longed-for closeness that is always to be
unfulfilled.

Apart from the Gibbsville and Hollywood tales,
Waiting for Winter contains other stories that deal with
diverse subjects and are of different kinds. They include a number of superior stories—the realistic,
haunted "Flight," in which an older playwright, past
the peak of his career, dies after a fall on the ice; and
"Andrea," about a young woman who, in the course of
a marriage and many affairs is unable to find herself,
and whose suicide at the end has the weird effect of an
optical illusion. "Andrea" encompasses a long period
of time, but "Assistant" takes place in the early hours
of a single morning. Maggie Muldoon, a much-married
nightclub singer on her way down awakens early in
her New York apartment and in the sequence that follows, through her recall of the past, her background is

filled out, leading to the expected arrival in an hour of Jimmy Rhodes. Rhodes is a man-about-town who has no taste and is "all wrong," but will provide her with a desperately needed anchorage. Maggie, whose morning vodkas are her "assistant" to get her through her day, remembers Rhodes's having brought her home the night before and, in a fogged way, his having said he would come back the next morning at seven. So she remembers, but when she goes into the living room and switches on the light she finds Rhodes dead on the couch. Dressed in a frilly shirt and tasseled shoes, he is still seated, staring straight ahead, as if waiting to be called into her bedroom. "The worst," O'Hara remarks in the final sentence, "was the eyes, seen through thick lenses."

O'Hara's versatility in *Waiting for Winter* may be illustrated by two final stories that are in every way different yet are both the work of a master—"The Jama" and "The General." "The Jama" is a suspenseful story about a widower who owns a yacht and has a man and woman on board who work for him and with whom he drinks—both hardened types, the woman flashily cheap. On shore, a man named Blair observes the yacht through a pair of binoculars and then goes out to the yacht to talk to the owner. The atmosphere on board is disturbing, and more disturbing still is Blair's final recognition that the owner may well be done away with by his employees before reaching his Florida destination. At the end, "The Jama" becomes another of O'Hara's imaginings of isolation.

One of the pleasures of "The Jama" is its carefully controlled and very gradual revelation of the yacht owner's frightening situation. "The General," on the other hand, is a smilingly ironic tale, told in a leisurely fashion and having no sense of peril whatever. O'Hara's manner could not be more urbane. This urbanity involves a continual play of irony over the principal fig-

ure, Dixon Hightower. Hightower is nominally a general, but this title has come to him through his
belonging to the National Guard, following his service
in World War I, where he never saw action. He married a wealthy woman, relieving him of the need to
work; and as the story opens his life is made up of a
ritual of small routines—mailing a letter at the post office, spending the afternoon at his club. Hightower is a
man, like Robert Millhouser in *Ourselves to Know*,
whom life has passed by.

One smiles at the futility of his life, his rather tim-
idly respectful devotion to outward forms and social
rituals. Later one smiles when, in the privacy of his
bedroom, Hightower is revealed as a transvestite. His
wearing of female garments to stimulate him into sexual relations with his wife is an amusingly fanciful idea,
and yet is made to seem plausible by the lonely and
bloodless nature of his life. The success of the story is
in the manner of its handling—O'Hara's superbly wry
humor, the deftness of his treatment of the general and
his sheltered, innocently compliant wife. O'Hara gives
the impression that he knows the couple to the life—
the genteel forms they observe, the halts in their
speech, the way they think, what they say to each
other in the bedroom. "The General" is the last word in
virtuosity in a story collection that reveals it at every
point.

And Other Stories (1968), a slighter volume than
Waiting for Winter, is the last collection of short stories
that O'Hara published during his lifetime. It contains
twelve stories, seven of which are set in "the Region,"
including one, "A Few Trips and Some Poetry," that is
a hundred and twenty pages long—approximately a
third of the book. Much the best of the grittily realistic
tales is "The Gunboat and Madge," the narrative of
which moves back and forth in time, beginning with
the appearance in Gibbsville of Jay Fitzpatrick, a

small-time prizefighter known as "the Gunboat." In the second round of a fixed fight the Gunboat is stretched on the canvas by the local boy, Kid Flynn; afterward, the two go out together to drink and visit the local "hoors." But it turns out that Jay is more fortunate than Kid Flynn who, late that night, has his throat slashed by "a fat and solemn Negro" in Colliery-ville. Jay becomes a bartender and bouncer at Bressler's saloon, where he steals steadily from his employer until, on Bressler's death, he buys the establishment from his widow.

The Gunboat's consort in Gibbsville is a woman named Madge who, after stealing from her employer, opens the La France Beauty Salon. Both dress flashily and frequent speakeasies; but although the Gunboat dreams of someday becoming "big," it is obvious that he and Madge have gone as far in life as they can go. At the end, the narrative leaps forward to the present as the Gunboat and Madge, now retired, celebrate their fortieth wedding anniversary in Florida, where they live. The Gunboat uses a cane, but is in fairly good health. Madge likes to sunbathe, wearing large sunglasses with rhinestones studding the rims. Her hair is dyed blue. O'Hara is present in this story in all his strength—in his earthy realism, his sly drollery, and the grotesqueness he brings to his characters' lives.

A striking feature of *And Other Stories* is the unusual degree of interest O'Hara shows in lesbianism—"a perplexing aspect," as Matthew Bruccoli has remarked, "of O'Hara's last phase." This concern appears in several of the stories, obliquely in "We'll Have Fun," and directly in the sophisticated and psychologically suspenseful "The Broken Giraffe." But it is treated most fully in the nouvelle-length story "A Few Trips and Some Poetry." The story is narrated by James Malloy, beginning at the time of his youth in Gibbsville and his romantic interest in Isabel Barley, a young Wellesley graduate living in nearby Turnersville. At one point they have sexual relations and know that they are not in love but, as Malloy says, "would be loving each other" for the rest of their lives.

"A Few Trips and Some Poetry" is a "life chronicle" that recounts, over a period of many years, the stages of their relationship and various reunions, of Isabel's two marriages, and her eventual adoption of a lesbian life. At the end, when both of them are a good deal older, Malloy calls on Isabel at her country house, shared with a younger woman with whom she has had a placid relationship and found a kind of peace. The younger woman, whom Malloy finds that he likes, idolizes Isabel. Isabel has not as yet told her, however, although she does tell Malloy when they talk together alone, that she has cancer, "is riddled with it." The ending, which has the form of a farewell, requires the most delicate handling, and is given it by O'Hara. He manages to create the mood of an idyll at the end, as love is approached but love-and-division becomes the final statement O'Hara has to make about life.

After O'Hara's death, fifty additional, uncollected stories were found among his papers at "Linebrook." Thirty-two of them were collected in *The Time Element and Other Stories* (1972), but this volume is made up entirely of stories from O'Hara's earlier period, almost all of them having been written in the 1940s. *Good Samaritan and Other Stories* (1974) is a slender volume containing fourteen stories written in the 1960s, twelve of them previously unpublished. Several of the stories in the volume compare with O'Hara's best. These include the title story, "Good Samaritan"; "The Gentry," a slowly paced, atmospheric tale set in a small Pennsylvania town; and "A Man to be Trusted," in which James Malloy, making his final appearance, recounts his relationship as a boy, and then later in life, with an attractive, older, married woman.

In this way, O'Hara's stories conclude as they began, with James Malloy, depicted as an adolescent in

"The Doctor's Son," a young reporter in *Butterfield 8*, a middle-aged man in later stories, a widower, and then a still older man who witnesses the death of his friends. In "A Man to be Trusted," in his last appearance, he is an adolescent again as the story opens, involved marginally with an older woman, but in such a way as to make the relationship impossible. An early sexual experience, followed by a sense of guilt, and the threat of reprisal (figured in the husband and the gun he carries) make the tale similar to O'Hara's first story, "The Doctor's Son," which is filled with sexual guilt and a projected sense of punishment. The first and last Malloy tales thus encompass much of O'Hara's other fiction, in which sex, guilt, punishment, and the burden of isolation are prominent themes.

Taken as a group, the later stories reveal a new richness and expansion of O'Hara's art. O'Hara is able to relax, as he previously could not, into the pleasures of extended observation, and as a psychologist of his characters' lives he has never been more acute or written with such grace. O'Hara is unapologetically graceful in these stories, capable of extraordinary delicacy of handling. At the same time he enlarges upon his themes—creates the life of modern suburbanites, of America's affluent class, of older characters who have to confront death, to surrender the last of their illusions. He is a raw realist, an elegant humorist, an ironist, an elegist, a virtuoso who has gained in confidence and poise. But what one notices most of all about these stories is that O'Hara has learned compassion, has treated his sufferers with generosity, and as equals with himself. The same is not true, however, of O'Hara's late novels, which are sometimes harsh and bitter in their view of life and show a preoccupation with extreme states of alienation. As the following chapter will indicate, O'Hara was provided with more "personalities" than even the many-sided late stories can contain.

7

The Late Novels:
The Spectrum from
Ourselves to Know to
The Ewings

O'Hara's final decade as a novelist was inaugurated by
Ourselves to Know (1960), which has the form partly
of a family chronicle, but is strikingly different from
O'Hara's family sagas of the 1950s in its extraordinary
interest in the inner life of its protagonist Robert Millhouser. If *Ourselves to Know* is psychological in its
orientation to a degree unwitnessed in O'Hara's earlier
novels, it is also more philosophic. It questions the relationship of God and man, the mysterious decrees of
fate and limitations placed upon individuals by their
psychic makeup. Robert Millhouser's life forms the
basis of a meditation not only on Millhouser but also
on the condition of mankind.

    Among the books O'Hara read just before writing
Ourselves to Know, two seem particularly relevant to
the novel. One was *The Education of Henry Adams*, in
which Adams pondered his personal fate as a man in
the nineteenth century, particularly his exclusion or
disqualification from the mainstream of American life.
Robert Millhouser came of age at the time of the Civil
War and belonged to Adams's generation; and he is
like Adams in being an educated man with a strong

tendency toward asceticism. Like Adams, too, the introverted Millhouser broods upon his life, is a biographer of his own experience, and has a view of the world that is almost unrelievedly pessimistic.

Another book O'Hara read at this time and that seemed to influence him was Edith Wharton's *Ethan Frome*. *Ethan Frome* is set very strongly in a particular region, the New England village of Starkfield and the drear, melancholy countryside surrounding it. *Ourselves to Know* also belongs to a distinct region, central eastern Pennsylvania, and more particularly the small town of Lyons; and although Lyons does not lie under as great a blight as does Starkfield, it is also somewhat out of the way, and the reclusive Millhouser seems as remote a figure in this setting as Ethan Frome had been in his. *Ethan Frome* and *Ourselves to Know* are distinctly similar in their narrative structures and in some essentials of their stories. Both begin with first-person narrators who inquire into the life of an individual cut off from the community proper; and in the background of both men a "terrible incident" has occurred that is still remembered or talked about by the inhabitants of their towns.

Ethan Frome and Robert Millhouser are alike particularly in their being closed in, in a particularly lonely way, upon themselves. The narrator of *Ethan Frome* remarks of the hero early in the novel, "I simply felt that he lived in a depth of moral isolation too remote for casual access," and Millhouser gives a similar impression. At a certain point, the narrators come to meet the heroes and act as their biographers, relating their stories to the reader. Wharton shifts at an early part of the work from the narrator-outsider to an informed narrator, able to reconstruct events as if present when they occurred. In *Ourselves to Know*, O'Hara also begins in the present with a narrator-outsider who goes back in time to recount what happened as if he himself had been present. In both novels, the reclusive heroes suffer severe repression and have emotionally starved lives. Violence finally breaks out in a dramatic incident, but instead of freeing the heroes from their isolation the incident merely commits them more terribly to it. They continue in their painful isolation with stoic endurance.

But if O'Hara begins with the narrative strategies of *Ethan Frome*, the complications he introduces make these strategies far more intricate than in Wharton; the narrative complexity of *Ourselves to Know*, in fact, exceeds anything in O'Hara's previous novels. The work, which covers a vast time span extending from the 1850s to 1944, is related in both the advancing present and the past, its reversions to the past achieved through a variety of means, including the long flashback. At certain points O'Hara even creates the sense of the simultaneity of time, as the presentness of the past is suddenly experienced by the narrator. The reconstruction of the past is made the more remarkable and intricate by the fact that, at certain points, there are not one but two narrators. Gerald Higgins is the essential narrator, but at times Millhouser himself assumes the narrator's role—sometimes in conversation, sometimes in lengthy letters he writes to Gerald, and once in a long account of a portion of his life that he sends to Gerald as a manuscript of biographical material.

The novel becomes a collaboration of narrators, and eventually the two narrators are brought together in a shared fate. The strategy O'Hara uses is similar to Joseph Conrad's use of narrator-observer and subject, like Marlowe and Kurtz in Conrad's *Heart of Darkness*, and the recognition the narrator makes at the end that the man he has been observing has some important relation to himself. The relationship of Millhouser and Gerald Higgins is also analogous to the relationship of

Gatsby and Nick Carraway, who is Gatsby's "biographer" in a sense, is drawn to Gatsby, attempts to understand his life, and in the end finds that Gatsby's
losses are also his own. Throughout *Ourselves to Know*
Gerald Higgins attempts to get at the heart of Millhouser's emotional and sexual incapacities, but at the
end, while serving in the navy during World War II, he
reveals that stories have got back to him about his
wife, and he, too, seems disabled and alone.

It comes out rather early in *Ourselves to Know*
that Robert Millhouser had murdered his wife, and
thus no suspense exists as to what the critical episode
was in Millhouser's life. The suspense of the novel lies
in knowing the how and why of it, in understanding
what the incident means in terms of Millhouser's un-
folding story. The murder does not occur until very
late in the work, and O'Hara leads up to it only very
gradually by focusing upon selected periods in Millhouser's life—his twenties and thirties, his marriage
and imprisonment, and the period following his release. Because the reader is informed early of the
murder, O'Hara is able to highlight later episodes of
Millhouser's life, such as the incidents following the
murder, out of chronological order.

What is particularly impressive about *Ourselves to
Know* is the psychological atmosphere that suffuses it.
From the moment he first appears, Robert Millhouser
is evoked as a haunted and solitary man, walking with
the sound of the Angelus bell against the traffic of men
on their way home to dinner. Rarely, in fact, does he
leave his large house "enclosed" by a white paling
fence at the edge of town. He is more confined within
the family house than Joe Chapin, in *Ten North Frederick*, is in his. Millhouser lives in the house with a single
companion, Moses Hatfield, a black man and old family retainer who is one of the novel's most finely drawn
characters. The house becomes virtually emblematic

of Millhouser's haunted mind, and in its morbid atmosphere and sense of a haunted isolation, it makes
one think of Hawthorne.

Early in the work, as an adolescent, Gerald Higgins stays in Lyons at the house of his grandfather,
Jeremiah MacMahon. There he observes Millhouser,
and later begins to ask questions about him. Later still,
when he is studying for his master's degree at Princeton,
he decides to write an account of Millhouser's life. The
project is begun, put aside, and picked up again over a
period of years. Millhouser is examined by Gerald
from many perspectives and at different points in
time, but there is still much about him that he is never
to learn. For one thing, Millhouser tells him only part
of his story, while withholding other information.
O'Hara insists that the enigma of Millhouser's nature
and incapacities ultimately defies full explanation, that
no one's life can ever be entirely understood.

Three characters, however, enter importantly into
and have an effect on Millhouser's life. The first is his
widowed mother, Zilph, a woman so self-contained
that she is temperamentally unable to show him love (a
role usually assigned in O'Hara to the father). Another
is Chester Calthorp, Millhouser's closest college friend,
a cultivated young man who wishes to become a painter,
as Millhouser does himself, and whom Millhouser
looks up to and admires. After college, Millhouser goes
to Rome with Calthrop to study painting; but there he
becomes homesick, recognizes that he has no gift as a
painter, and, what is more, discovers that Calthorp is
an active homosexual. Disillusioned, Millhouser returns home, where he lives with his mother until her
death in 1902. Essentially he is alone. Years pass in this
way until he meets the third person to affect him deci-
sively, Hedwig Steele.

At the time Millhouser marries Hedwig, or
Hedda, Steele, he is fifty-one and she is eighteen. The

daughter of a widely traveled engineer who has recently moved to Lyons, she is quite beautiful, and Millhouser sees her as a last chance to "eradicate loneliness,
or anaesthetize it." Millhouser does not see her clearly,
but Hedda has a very sharp sense of him, as can be
seen when she compares him in her mind to a small
"altar boy" she had once noticed in a foreign country.
Hedda is an extraordinary conception—more de-
praved in youth than Mary St. John Eaton, in *From the
Terrace*, is in maturity. In a striking passage, when the
Steeles are traveling by train in South America, Hedda
does not occupy herself with picture books but stares
brazenly at fellow passengers. She seduces a much
older man, who later hangs himself, and in Mexico
City, when her mother lets her out of her sight, she has
an affair with a Johnny Villareal. When her mother
slaps her, Hedda slaps back. Hedda is the "bad seed"
the Steeles have somehow produced, and in Lyons
they are more than willing to transfer their daughter in
matrimony to the much older Millhouser. After the
marriage, they move away.

Robert Millhouser is a wealthy man, the director
of an important bank, and he has much to offer
Hedda. What he gives, she takes. But nothing can satisfy
this demonic child. She demands sex from him insatia-
bly, but after a time, as O'Hara comments, "his thin
lips were not the lips she wanted on her." During the
first year of the marriage, she has an affair with the
crudely physical Bart Vance, who sees her late at night
at the house when Millhouser is away on business.
These incidents so trouble the servants that they give
notice, and finally, learning of her relations with
Vance, Millhouser reaches the point where he knows
that he must kill her. He shoots her in her bed as she
sleeps. O'Hara implies that Millhouser had married
Hedda because he had known subconsciously that
something terrible would come of the marriage, and
that this would bring him out of his isolation by forcing

him to *feel*. But even after committing the worst of human acts, the taking of another's life, he remains "devoid of feeling," and in killing Hedda, who represents the passional part of experience, he removes himself forever from life.

Robert Millhouser is presented with such elaborate indirection and is such an elusive figure that one wonders if there is not some trick involved in O'Hara's creation of him. Many indicators in the novel suggest that he is latently homosexual, but if so then at least part of the enigma of his nature is dispelled. Millhouser's most important male friendship is with Chester Calthrop, of whose homosexuality there is no question, and their lives have important parallels. Calthorp explores his homosexuality in Italy and, after reaching a cul-de-sac, adopts the life of a monk; Millhouser appears to spend his life dodging his homosexuality, but is led into an isolation even more profound than his friend's.

O'Hara himself makes the reader question Millhouser's sexual orientation. He does not have his first sexual experience until he is twenty-seven, when he goes to a prostitute who, despite the act, asks him if he is a "fairy." The small circle of homosexuals in Lyons, O'Hara notes, "had been quite convinced that Robert belonged with them and would respond with the slightest beckoning." Furthermore, O'Hara has at several points associated Millhouser with Henry James, whose psychological inwardness and "incapacity for life" seem related to a severely repressed homosexuality. "He was an admirer, I suspect," Gerald Higgins remarks of Millhouser, "of the late Henry James. His prose style was similar to, if not imitative of, James's travel essays, which had been written at almost the same time that Robert Millhouser and Chester Calthorp were visiting some of the cities—Paris, Rome, Florence."

The house where the elusive Millhouser lives

with an ethnic companion, has a strongly, even morbidly, homoerotic atmosphere. After the tragedy,
there are no women in Millhouser's life, and there were
few before his marriage to Hedda. His most important
association in his later years is with another male,
Gerald Higgins, who becomes his amanuensis and
biographer. This association, whether intended by
O'Hara or not, has homosexual overtones. An intense
bonding takes place between them, so that at one
point Gerald feels that he and Millhouser have become
one. "I was still so young," Gerald writes, "that my
smaller life was fitting into his larger [one], sometimes
as though my life were like those surgical stitches that
had become part of the patient's flesh." In another passage, Gerald grows drowsy while talking to Millhouser
at his house, and Millhouser suggests that he may wish
to take a nap. Gerald then goes up to Millhouser's
room, and sleeps on the bed where the murder had occurred, wearing Millhouser's pajamas. In this scene,
and in others, O'Hara uses the device of the character
double, but its sexual implications are nevertheless
striking.

The problem of how Robert Millhouser should be
regarded, whether as a man incapacitated for life because he cannot "feel," or as a man who can be explained partly as a repressed homosexual, troubles the
novel, although it does not destroy it. Millhouser is a
richly evoked character, projected dramatically and
memorably against the background of his blighted
past and isolation in his morbidly moldering house in
Lyons; and even if uncertain of its causes, the reader is
wholly convinced of his paralysis. *Ourselves to Know*
reveals O'Hara's talent at maturity—in his rich creation
of the community of Lyons, his many convincingly
drawn characters, and emphasis upon the projection
of sensibility over outward events. It ranks with *Ten
North Frederick* as a novel that possesses a depth of
imaginative engagement with its subject and situation.

In the same year that O'Hara published *Ourselves to Know*, he also published *Sermons and Soda-Water* (1960), the title of which derives from Byron's *Don Juan*: "Let us have wine and women, mirth and laughter,/Sermons and soda-water the day after." The title is actually ironic, since what the volume deals with is the passing of youth, the middle-aged aftermath of happier times. *Sermons and Soda-Water* is a collection of three nouvelles rather than a novel, but it can be discussed here briefly because it reflects O'Hara's preoccupations at the beginning of the 1960s decade. It has in common with *Ourselves to Know* that it is ostensibly "biographical," with the difference that in this case the narrator of all three nouvelles is James Malloy, O'Hara's recurring persona. Malloy's resemblance to O'Hara himself is so strong that the reader might be inclined to believe that these "fictions" come out of O'Hara's personal experience, a calculated effect that creates a sense of verisimilitude.

"The Girl on the Baggage Truck," the first of the nouvelles, is concerned with Malloy's friendship at different points in his life with the actress Sally Sears. It begins in the present in New York, when Malloy, working as a movie press agent, first meets Sally; it then moves back and forth in time, from 1930 to the present, as the narrative follows the actress when she is descending from the peak of her career, to her eclipse for many years following an auto wreck, to her comeback in films in old age. An engaging feature of "The Girl on the Baggage Truck" is O'Hara's chivalrous and understanding treatment of Sally, but the nouvelle is flawed in many ways. One of its major characters, for example, a mysterious financier named Hunterden, remains vague and unconvincing. The later section contains a remarkable scene, set at the North Shore estate of "Junior" Williamson, whose Yale background, great wealth, and arrogance give him an affinity with Tom Buchanan in *The Great Gatsby*. But this fine scene has little to do with the rest of the work, which seems disjointed and only partially realized.

"Imagine Kissing Pete," the best of the nouvelles, is Malloy's reminiscence of Barbara ("Bobbie") Hammersmith and Pete McCrea, with whom he had come of age in Gibbsville. It begins in 1929 when Bobbie Hammersmith, one of the belles of the town, and the daughter of a well-to-do independent coal operator, has been "in and out of love with all of us," but marries Pete McCrea. The story unfolds in a series of incidents in which Malloy revisits the old town to encounter the McCreas at various points in their marriage. Their movement socially is distinctly downward, as Bobbie's parents lose their money in the Depression and Pete comes to operate a pool hall that is connected with a numbers operation headed by the younger brother of Ed Charney, who had appeared in *Appointment in Samarra*. In the course of many years, the McCreas have a reconciliation in their shaky marriage and rise to the level of the middle class. In the final commencement scene their son graduates with honors from Princeton, an emotional moment that also signals the end of their marriage in a sense, since the son's departure from their lives forecasts a long period of aftermath in which Bobbie and Pete will no longer be as close or have as much to live for as, for a time, they had. The story is effective in its lower-class realism and close observation of human limitations—projected at the end with a sharp, clear emotion.

"We're Friends Again," the final nouvelle, is slight, and is essentially a tone poem about late middle age. Its plot rambles, and certain characters, such as Polly Williamson and Juliana Moore, enter the account without any clear sense of what they are doing there, or of how they relate exactly to the other characters. But the psychological atmosphere of the story is interesting. "We're Friends Again" is full of mood at the beginning when Malloy, now a widower, paces about his club in New York where he lives alone—an empty, ghostly place on a summer Sunday night, where the ticking of clocks can be heard distinctly, an intimation of the passing of time and the imminence of death. The nouvelle is filled with the sense of death and personal loss, and Malloy is portrayed as being the most solitary of men. He speaks of his "chronic loneliness," and at the end declares that loneliness and solitude are "the final condition of us all." All three nouvelles in the volume are meditations on the effect of time on people who, whether in friendship, marriage, or widowerhood, must be alone.

Sermons and Soda-Water is a slight work that yet contains some very fine moments, but O'Hara's novel *The Big Laugh* (1962) is disappointing to the point of being dismaying. In this novel, which gives the impression that it was improvised from the opening page to the final one, O'Hara returns to Hollywood, where he traces the career of an actor named Hubert Ward, an unsympathetic antihero. Hubert Ward is a kind of Pal Joey who succeeds, and he is like Joey in that his shallowness and opportunism are matched by the same qualities in the people around him. An out-of-work young man with good looks and a bad character, Hubert Ward drifts into acting in summer stock and, because he attracts the interest of a "double-gaited" producer named Martin Ruskin, is elevated to a part in a Broadway play. He receives favorable reviews and soon goes from New York to Hollywood, where he becomes a rising star. In the middle period of his career, when he marries Nina Stephens, he leads a quietly conventional life and his studio even uses him as a symbol of respectability within the profession. When his marriage founders, however, he reverts to type. A wealthy film idol and American legend at the end, he is as cynical and empty a being as he had been at the beginning.

The Big Laugh has been given what little structure

it has by the several phases of Hubert Ward's career, but even if it had been more structured it would still be deeply unsatisfactory. For one thing, Hubert Ward is a blank, has neither inner life nor outward plausibility. He does not even have the specialized kind of sensitivity that an actor, presumably, would need to have. That Hubert Ward, who has had no interest in the theatre nor any training, could come in off the street, appear in a Broadway play almost the next day, and be compared by drama critics to Alfred Lunt, is incredible. Similarly, it is not possible to believe in the various stages of his personal development. How, after all, could this hostile, antisocial personality ever have become a model, contented citizen during his middle period? Other characters in the novel are also not provided with plausible motivation. Nina Stephens, who is set apart from the others by her breeding, taste, and character, is depicted as becoming bored by Hubert when he becomes respectable, so that their marriage begins to come apart; but her boredom with a responsible husband is wholly out of character for her. Worse still is O'Hara's handling of Martin Ruskin, a contrived character both when he appears at the beginning and when he turns up again, melodramatically, at the end. The failure of motivation in these characters suggests a fatigued and exhausted imagination.

At one point only does *The Big Laugh* engage the reader—when Hubert is introduced to the circle of the high-ranking producer Charley Simmons and his wife Mildred, a situation somewhat similar to Fitzgerald's in his story "Crazy Sundays." At this point, the novel begins to be *about* something—the social structure of Hollywood society. The parties given at the executive level reveal the status of the various characters who belong to the film industry, and O'Hara notes their differences in status tellingly. Moreover, he has captured these characters in an evocative atmosphere of malaise that lies beneath the surface of their glittering success. Dialogue in this section is quite brilliant, and one of the characters, Mildred Simmons, is strongly felt, is a superior and fully realized character conception. But this middle portion of the novel disintegrates before long, and O'Hara returns to Hubert's meretricious success story, an account so artificial that it possesses very little sense of reality. What is striking about *The Big Laugh* ultimately is its hostile view of humanity, its embittered nihilism that also seems O'Hara's.

To move from *The Big Laugh* to *Elizabeth Appleton* (1963) is to come suddenly into the presence of sweet reasonableness. *Elizabeth Appleton* began as a play, entitled *The Sisters* or *You Are My Sister,* that O'Hara wrote in 1954, and its opening and conclusion, in which all the loose ends are tied together neatly, correspond to the opening and final acts of a play. *Elizabeth Appleton* is an "academic novel" of a kind, but not entirely. Its academic setting is less important to the novel than it might seem; and in addition the academics who appear in it are few and faint. Essentially, it is an inquiry into a marriage that is set against the background of a college in Pennsylvania.

The novel begins invitingly with the arrival from out of town of Elizabeth Appleton's sister Jean Roberts, and with the opening view of the Appleton house, a red-brick edifice that is "substantial, comfortable, respectable"—a solidly middle- rather than upper-class home. Jean's arrival is followed by the scene of a cocktail party at the house, where a number of local people associated with Spring Valley College or belonging to the community have been invited. They include Brice and Evangeline Ditson, local aristocrats; Brice's brother Porter Ditson, who dresses with panache and does not "care" to work or need to; and an eccentric professor emeritus named Hillenkitter, who wears a Vandyke beard and admits to owning a large collection of pornography. The scene is splendidly rendered and, intriguingly, many questions are raised as to the role these characters are to play in the work. The most critical question is whether John Appleton, formerly professor of American history and now dean, will be appointed to fill the vacancy as president of Spring Valley College.

By the end of chapter one, the reader is informed that he will not, but by then suspense about the appointment has been replaced by a suspenseful curiosity to know more about the Appletons and their situation. As in a number of his other novels, O'Hara drops back in time through a long flashback that moves steadily forward in time as it fills in the background and experience of the main characters. The final chapter takes up seamlessly where the first chapter left off, and provides a resolution of the drama—the acceptance by John and Elizabeth Appleton of each other and of their lives. *Elizabeth Appleton* is quite unlike O'Hara's other novels in its ending, which actually seems to endorse a rational accommodation to the world as it is.

Elizabeth Appleton reads in many respects like a novel of manners—without having the social density of one. It contains acute observations and is attentive to the social relationships of its characters, who are frequently defined by the class to which they belong. Elizabeth and her sister Jean, daughters of a Wall Street banker, have been brought up among the affluent on the North Shore of Long Island. Money is an important factor in their upbringing, since it dictates which individuals qualify and which do not. Elizabeth's mother, Amelia Webster, is a great aristo who comments with disapproval on the Prince of Wales's accessibility during a visit, his "extraordinarily democratic behavior on the North Shore." She distinctly does not favor Elizabeth's interest in young John Appleton, who is about to begin a teaching career at

Spring Valley College. Her husband, on the other hand, although he has made a good deal of money, has the attitudes of a leisured gentleman who sees beyond mere money-making and the artificial ranking of individuals by their incomes, and he endorses John Appleton as a husband for Elizabeth. Jarvis and Amelia Webster had had a son who drowned one summer in his youth, and Jarvis tends to see Appleton as a son, or as a replacement for the son he has lost. The Websters' marriage is not happy, and O'Hara implies that in securing Elizabeth's marriage to Appleton, Jarvis Webster has also taken revenge on his wife, whose snobbish attitudes have oppressed him. Elizabeth comes to John Appleton partly as the result of a conflict within the Webster family.

In her life with a history instructor, Elizabeth has had to conceal her wealthy background to ward off envy and hostility within the middle-class college community. With the death of her parents, she inherits four hundred thousand dollars, but would have the community believe that the inheritance was much smaller. She shops thriftily and lives without ostentation. Her adjustment to her husband's circumstances, however, is not total; and in certain ways she is quietly a subversive. She sends her son to St. Paul's and her daughter to Farmington, schools for the children of the economically advantaged, because she does not want them to remain in or belong to the world of Spring Valley. Inevitably, she has an affair; and since it is with a man of her own class, the leisured Porter Ditson, the affair is a kind of protest against the middle-class marriage she has made. The implication of her attraction to Porter Ditson is deepened when her sister Jean meets him and tells Elizabeth that he is "more like Father than anyone else I've met in years." Elizabeth takes her sister into her confidence, telling her that she has had an affair—now over—with Porter, and Jean remarks, "It would have had to be someone like that. Your way of going back to Southampton." *Elizabeth Appleton* is classical in the symmetry of many of its character relationships, and it ends sensibly with Elizabeth's remaining with her husband, although he is considerably less than the man he could be. At the end Elizabeth advises Jean, who has gone through her large inheritance and had two unsuccessful marriages, to think of settling down, of bringing her early expectations on the North Shore down to the level of ordinary life.

O'Hara's structuring of *Elizabeth Appleton* is handled skillfully, but the novel can be faulted in a number of respects, particularly in regard to characters who do not fill out their roles. The college's retiring president, Bruce McAndrews, has nothing to do in the novel except to meditate on how he can block John Appleton's appointment as his successor. This turns out to be unnecessary since the decision about the appointment is not even his. Barbara Speacht, whom McAndrews plans to marry after his retirement, thus wedding his academic prestige to her newly made money, is more of an anomaly still. She makes inquiries about Elizabeth's marriage and, incredibly, learns that a woman fitting her description used to visit Porter Ditson at one of her rental properties in Fort Penn; but she then fades from the work, never to be heard from again. In a somewhat similar way, Hillenkitter, the eccentric professor, appears in the novel but has no real function in it. Nor does Jean Roberts, a well-drawn character who promises to enlarge but does not, and whose only function at the end is to receive advice from her sister.

The novel has other limitations. Its collegiate background is relatively thin, and in the sequence that deals with the fraternity initiation, and the student demonstration before the Appleton house when it is learned that John is not to be named president, the writing is unconvincing. Troubling, too, is the arbitrary decision of the trustees to find someone from outside, an anticlimax that cancels out the impression the whole novel gives that the outcome will be determined by the complications existing among its characters. On the whole, however, *Elizabeth Appleton* is a rather agreeable, low-keyed work. It contains particularly acute observations of women, who have been more finely felt and are consistently more interesting than the novel's men. The ending is quiet, but one feature of it is striking—the revelation that Elizabeth has chosen to remain with John Appleton because he is weak and needs her even more than does Porter Ditson. A face-less, voiceless man of limited vision, John Appleton is something like Joe Chapin, but escapes his fate because the strong woman in his life chooses to spare him. In this respect, *Elizabeth Appleton* is a more smiling version of O'Hara's repeated theme of the man who is dominated or even emasculated by the woman he marries.

Elizabeth Appleton is placid in its interest in sensibility and social relationships, but the novel that follows it, *The Lockwood Concern* (1965), is surprisingly romantic, even at times baroque. As a multigenerational family chronicle, *The Lockwood Concern* might have been one of O'Hara's largest works, but has instead been kept to the proportions of a novel of medium length. It begins in the present, but before long, in O'Hara's familiar manner, goes back in time to the distant past, in this case to the career of the founding member of the family, Moses Lockwood, whose story begins in the period of Jeffersonian democracy of the 1830s. A cash-box thief, Moses Lockwood is ordered to leave one Pennsylvania town, but in another, Swedish Haven, near Gibbsville, he becomes a rich man. His nature is cunning, predatory, and secretive. He builds a brick house in the country, surrounded by a wall eight feet tall and surmounted by iron spikes, that resembles a "penitentiary." Like Moses in the Old Testament, he is a prophet, a seer, a man who fathers a chosen tribe and is possessed by a vision of its future greatness.

His son Abraham avoids service in the Civil War to commence his career in business, and is a more educated version of his father. Seemingly less ruthless in his business practices, he is actually no less alert to ways by which to advance himself. Trained from his early years by his father, he is able to expand the family holdings, and is obsessed by the idea of the "Lockwood Concern." "It was a Concern, in the Quaker sense of the term," O'Hara writes. "Although he was not a Quaker, he had heard of the Concern, which was the name given to an obsessive act or thought, or both, of a religious nature. . . . Abraham Lockwood's Concern was with the establishment of a dynasty of his own line."

In the third generation, George Lockwood has a new brick house built just outside Swedish Haven. It is surrounded by a brick wall surmounted by iron spikes, in the manner of his grandfather's. In craft and cunning, George goes even further than did Moses Lockwood, for he has a secret passageway, a circular staircase running from his bedroom to his study below, to the cellar, built into the house by Italian laborers. In a Gothic manner, a gargoyle in the bedroom closet, when turned like a doorknob, releases the door to the staircase. Although the lives of the Lockwoods are related with the density of closely specified social fact, the novel is not entirely a work of realism, being more nearly a romance novel. It is a work of excess, the whole manner of which adumbrates the excessive nature of the Lockwood Concern which, in language virtually Melvillian, O'Hara calls an "obsession. A purpose. A mania."

O'Hara called *The Lockwood Concern* "an old fashioned morality," a fair enough description of it in its continual consciousness of good and evil, and the lesson that runs all through it that the price of moral isolation is death. Death enters thematically into such earlier novels as *Appointment in Samarra* and *Ten North Frederick*, and into many of O'Hara's stories of the 1960s concerned with characters who are aging. But in *The Lockwood Concern* death is a constant presence and comes to seem like the ultimate reality that the Lockwoods, in their hereditary obsession, are attempting to outrun. Death is associated with the line's founder Moses Lockwood, who had killed two men, and with many of the Lockwood women, who are blighted in their lives, or waste away and die. When George Lockwood's house is completed, a boy from nearby who has climbed a tree limb to peer over the wall falls to his death, impaled on the spikes along the top of the wall; and his death seems an ill omen for the future of the house. When his brother Penrose commits suicide, George Lockwood dissociates himself from the incident, determined not to let it deter him from his self-aggrandizing ambitions. He lies down to rest at this point "in a position that had the formality of death, his arms straight down at his sides, his legs stretched full length, inescapably reminiscent of cadavers in a morgue." At the very end of the novel, George Lockwood dies in a fall on the secret staircase. Alone in his death agony in the empty depths of the house he built, blinded and choking on his vomit as he attempts to cry out, he seems like some terrible sufferer in hell.

The Lockwood house is the opening and final setting of *The Lockwood Concern,* but it appears as well in other sections of the novel, and is ever present in the reader's mind. It holds the family's moral history, its egotism, and terrible isolation from others. Human isolation is, of course, O'Hara's great theme; but in *The*

Lockwood Concern it has been treated more romantically than elsewhere, and has been given a distinctive
psychological emphasis. What lies behind the "Concern," really, is paranoia. The Lockwoods' paranoiac
mind can be noticed in their extreme, unnatural suspiciousness of others, the defenses they raise to keep
others away from them, and the grandiose schemes
and sense of themselves that they nurture. However
baroque George Lockwood's life may be, it is focused
by a believable "mind set," and to know George
Lockwood is to enter memorably into the imagination
of paranoia. The fantasia of his mind has been created
at a level of excitement that exceeds anything in *Elizabeth Appleton,* and despite its oddness, melodrama,
and excess, it is a more deeply imagined novel.

Vaguely, and even though O'Hara condemns him,
one has the sense that there is something of O'Hara in
George Lockwood. In the seclusion of his study at
"Linebrook," remote from the outer world, O'Hara
was driven by work as obsessively as his father had
been. Like George Lockwood, O'Hara was a high
achiever whose very achievement had entailed isolation which, through Lockwood, he has imagined as the
most terrible of sins. Sin, guilt, and punishment are
acted out in Lockwood's life; and it is as if through his
hero O'Hara has projected some of his innermost anxieties. It was at "Linebrook" that O'Hara wrote *Ourselves to Know* and *The Lockwood Concern,* psychological studies of men who are enclosed within their
substantial houses and are made to suffer the fate of a
terrible isolation. What is interesting about Robert Millhouser and George Lockwood, too, is that they both
have some affinity with the artist. Millhouser is a failed
painter and torturously introspective man who is compared to Henry James, and although Lockwood is ostensibly a hero of business, what is striking about him
is that he lives almost entirely within his own mind, as

a writer might live alone with his conceptions. Both of these men, who give some suggestion of the artist or writer, are punished by O'Hara and made to suffer torment. In the novel that follows *The Lockwood Concern*, *The Instrument* (1967), O'Hara's hero is a writer literally, a man who cannot relate deeply to others because of some obscure emotional maiming experienced early in his life, with the result that his most personal relationships are merely grist for the mill of his creative process.

The antihero of *The Instrument* is Robert Yancey ("Yank") Lucas, a young playwright who, before coming to New York, had been unable to establish any communication with his father, a professor of art history at Spring Valley College, and had been married, unhappily, to a young woman who had betrayed him with her infidelity. These two experiences are the only explanation O'Hara gives for Yank's bitter recoil from people, his tremendous self-enclosure that O'Hara, as a moralist, has associated with death. *The Instrument* opens on a scene of near death, when Yank, living alone in a shabby tenement in New York, is revived by a neighbor after gas has filled his apartment. Yank then writes the experience into his play, which is before long presented successfully on the stage. This incident establishes a pattern for him throughout the novel. When he becomes involved with Zena Gollum, who stars in his play, and then abandons her to her fate so that he may brood on his next play in the isolation of the Vermont countryside, she commits suicide. He is not the cause of her death, but he has a certain share of responsibility in it. What she means to him chiefly is seen in his use of her in his new play. Her forfeited life is the "life" behind his play. At the end, O'Hara indicates that Yank must now feed on others for his future conceptions, like a vampire.

As always, even in his weaker works, O'Hara

creates social surfaces with a mesmerizing facility. His main characters in *The Instrument* who belong to the theatre are established immediately with their rough Broadway talk, and one of them, Peg McInerney, a theatrical agent who is gustier and more obscene in her speech than the men, is a delightful conception. Once beautiful and in many a man's bed, she is now middle-aged and overweight. She is solaced by the companionship of young men on the fringes of the theatre whom she has on a leash; is a seasoned professional who talks constantly and knows everything; and is surprisingly and disarmingly likable. About a third of the way through the novel, O'Hara shifts his setting to rural Vermont, where other minor characters are encountered, a number of them—like Anna Phelps and the wealthy Atterbury couple—delicately and suggestively created.

O'Hara is less successful, however, with his main characters. Zena Gollum, who is supposed to represent "life," and was possibly inspired by Marilyn Monroe (in her marriage to the playwright Arthur Miller), has no depth of reality or even personal distinctness, and it is difficult to see how she could have given Yank's play its "life." Yank's two plays, in fact, one presented to acclaim in New York and the other, only just finished at the end, are always remote from the reader and seem somewhat unreal. Moreover, the reader has only O'Hara's word for it that Yank is a playwright at all, since his cerebration takes place out of the reader's sight. Chiefly, he seems numbed in his anger and conviction that the world is loathsome and meaningless. At one point he calls himself "emotionally impotent," which places him in a line of descent from Robert Millhouser, who cannot "feel," and George Lockwood, who can feel only the paranoiac throb of the "Concern," and like them he is distinctly neurotic. Had he been brought more fully to life, *The Instrument* might have been a realized novel rather than the sketch for one that it is.

Like *The Instrument, Lovey Childs: A Philadelphian's Story* (1969) is distinguished by a disdainful view of humanity. The idea of this short novel is fairly simple. As a young girl, Charlotte Lewis, known as "Lovey," is anxious to come of age, to join the adult world; but her initiation into it is a horror, and when, at the end, people ask why she has remained with her second husband, with whom she has little in common, the reader understands that her marriage is a shelter from the storm of life. As in a series of O'Hara's previous novels, the family house in *Lovey Childs* has a symbolic function. It is a large house with servants, part of Pennsylvania's Main Line society, and represents considerable wealth and apparent security. Even at the beginning, however, following the death of Lovey's father, who has lost much of his money through poor investments, the house is in jeopardy. It seems to shrink as its acreage is sold off parcel by parcel, and this shrinkage accompanies Lovey's growth to maturity, the scaling down and finally the loss of her illusions.

A pronounced feature of *Lovey Childs* is its concern with lesbianism, which also appears in a number of O'Hara's stories of the 1960s. In *Lovey Childs*, although not in all the stories, lesbianism is treated as if it were a diseased aberration of sexuality. Lovey's mother is revealed as a lesbian, and her mental breakdown, which occurs after her seduction of a young girl in Buffalo, New York, is made to seem directly attributable to her sexual orientation. Another character, Marcy Bancroft, a lesbian student with Lovey at the Hathaway school, is almost preternaturally evil, a character similar in her precocious carnal knowledge to the "imp child" Hedda in *Ourselves to Know*. Moreover, when Lovey is in Reno obtaining a divorce from her first husband Sky Childs, she is stalked and seduced by Virginia Vernon, a confirmed lesbian and a very unpleasant individual. Lesbianism is implied in other parts of the work as well (in the girls at the first school Lovey attends and in Ida Van Fleet Roberts, headmistress of the Hathaway school), and its "sinister" shadow stretches across the novel.

Sex itself in *Lovey Childs*, in whatever form, seems peculiarly diseased. Sky Childs, the sportsman-millionaire Lovey marries, loses no time in being unfaithful to her with a show girl. The sleazy details of their divorce, splashed across the pages of the New York tabloids, make it clear that the marriage was not made in heaven. In another instance of the unloveliness of sex, Henry Gage, a socialite, has his throat slashed in Harlem, where he had gone one night in search of offbeat pleasure. The novel is set for the most part in the late 1920s and the early part of the Great Depression, and its sexual theme is intended to evoke the bankruptcy of the period. Many other Main Line families, as well as Lovey's, are tarnished by scandal or go under financially during this time. Lovey's story might even have had a certain plausibility if O'Hara had not continually resorted to melodramatic devices. It is incredible, for example, that Lovey's mother, a woman who seems eminently stable when she first appears, should, when the reader hears of her again, be confined to a mental institution as the result of a lesbian strain in her makeup. It is preposterous that Lovey should seduce Father McIldowney when he comes to look at the Lewis home as a possible property for the Church, and that he should later hang himself from a rafter in the sacristy. Such instances of melodramatic plotting as these destroy any claim to seriousness that the work might have, and make *Lovey Childs* one of O'Hara's emptiest novels.

In some respects, *Lovey Childs* reads like a preliminary sketch for O'Hara's last, posthumously published novel *The Ewings* (1972), which also shows a pronounced preoccupation with lesbianism. Ada Ewing, a married woman and mother who discovers her lesbianism, is a more fortunate version of Dorothy Lewis, Lovey's mother; and Grafton Williams, the family lawyer, longtime personal friend and counselor in *Lovey Childs*, inspires Clarence Kelley. Grafton Williams is the one real success in character drawing in *Lovey Childs*. He is the kind of upright, older professional man who always wears a vest, and yet when confronted with the aberrations occurring within the Lewis family is surprisingly undismayed and understanding. Clarence Kelly, in *The Ewings*, has these same qualities, but is a figure of larger size than Grafton Williams. Rather than remaining a marginal character, he enters importantly into the novel, becoming one of the finest and most sensitively captured characters in the work.

The Ewings did not deserve the uniformly hostile reviews it received when it appeared, but it clearly has many flaws. Its structure, for one thing, is not altogether satisfactory. Bill Ewing was supposedly based on a government cabinet member, and *The Ewings* begins as if it were to recount the story of a young man who is to rise to a position of considerable importance. A number of the scenes are concerned with the world of business and finance—with the Cleveland law firm of Hotchkiss, Ewing & Kelley, where Bill Ewing succeeds his late father as a partner while he is still in his late twenties, and with the Cuyahoga Iron and Steel Company, to which Ewing is named to a directorship. Yet it soon develops that the real subject of the novel is Bill Ewing's mother Ada, who takes over the work. Bill Ewing's career is just getting underway when the novel ends, and the reader has the sense that the work contains an undeveloped story, is more of an opening episode than a completed novel. That O'Hara, at the

time of his death, had begun work on a sequel, tenta-
tively entitled *The Second Ewings*,[1] confirms this
impression.

More serious faults can be found in O'Hara's characterizations. Priscilla Hotchkiss is a character who,
like Mary St. John Eaton in *From the Terrace*, changes
her nature midway in the work. She is revealed at the
end as a cheap young woman, interested cynically
only in sex, but the earlier part gives no suggestion of
the depth of vulgarity imputed to her later. Her husband is a junior partner in a prestigious law firm, and
although he does not appear, what is said about him
makes him seem so unstable that it is difficult to see
how he could carry on his work, much less be in line
for a partnership. George Barr, when he appears near
the end, is thinly and unconvincingly created, a cursed
papier-mâché homosexual. These characters are cretins,
have no depth to them as people, and have been
created by O'Hara with no attempt at reality. It is as if
they had been "put in" by O'Hara, whether plausible
or not, to emphasize his theme of the deepening isolation and loneliness of his characters.

Yet O'Hara is distinctly more successful with his
two major characters, Ada Ewing and Clarence Kelley.
Early in the novel, O'Hara introduces the theme of
sexual repression and loneliness in pre–World War I
America, illustrated by the lives of many of his characters. Ada Ewing has been a proper wife of a successful
Cleveland attorney, and later as a widow at fifty-two
she discovers that her life has kept her in ignorance not
only of the world but even of herself. What is conspicuous about Ada is not that she is a dissolute woman but
that she is an innocent. There is an odd kind of humor
in O'Hara's treatment of her—so odd that it is hard
even to characterize. It involves irony, but is not
harshly sardonic. "Playful" and "whimsical" are words
that come to mind, but they do not quite capture

O'Hara's "all-knowing" quality in regard to her, his almost mysterious refraining from expressing an overt attitude toward her. O'Hara always knows much more than Ada does, both about herself and about the different social groups she enters. In Ada's initiation into lesbian sexuality with Priscilla, her responses are almost childlike in their simplicity; she is genuinely surprised that such practices exist and that they give tactile pleasure, and at the same time she remains somehow matronly and well-behaved. When she confides her experiences to Clarence Kelley and he speaks of "lesbianism," she tells him, in all candor, that she has never before heard the word.

Later, Ada goes to visit her wealthy friend Sophie Cudlipp at Palm Springs and discovers that Sophie, also a widow, keeps a handsome younger man named Will Levering. One night Levering steals into Ada's room to make love to her, obviously a "present" from Sophie, and her horizons are expanded, although she continues to be naive. After she has been back in Cleveland, and scandal begins to spread about her rather marginal relations with Priscilla, Ada finds it best to get away. She visits her old school friend Rhoda Shipley, a wealthy widow in Santa Barbara, and in a scene that is handled with a suave understatement by O'Hara, they find that they have both been lonely and have a common lesbian interest. The two matrons, a little over fifty, find their solution to loneliness in living together as lovers. At the end, her name darkened by scandal in Cleveland, Ada seems every bit as unworldly as she had appeared at the beginning. Ada is an unlikely conception, yet she lives as a character as many of the minor characters do not; and she has been treated with a generosity that O'Hara has also accorded Clarence Kelley.

Clarence Kelley is somewhat off to the side of the novel in the earlier part, but in an unpredictable strategy, O'Hara makes him the focal figure of the work at the end. He, too, has had an unfulfilled life. After a relationship with a young man that threatens to become talked about, he marries unhappily, and later forms a platonic fondness for Bill Ewing's father. After Kelley's death, his life is suddenly made more clear to the reader. Bill Ewing enters Kelley's bedroom, which contains his books—including volumes of Freud, Walt Whitman, and *Huck Finn*—and, with an irony of which he is not aware, remarks: "What a lonely life he must have led!" He then notices and is puzzled by an old photograph of his parents, taken fifteen years before, on their boat *The Wanderer*, and wonders why Kelley had kept it in his bedroom for years. Suspecting that the admirable Clarence Kelley had loved his mother, he is swayed to think less harshly of her, and the novel ends with a poignant sense of the distances that divide people.

In the 1960s, O'Hara produced a staggering amount of work—eight short story collections, seven novels, and several nouvelles, as well as plays and screen scenarios and a large amount of nonfiction.[2] He worked incessantly, without revising what he wrote; had he done so, his weakest work at least would surely have benefited. But as it is, the period adds to his achievement. To his superior earlier work in the novel— *Appointment in Samarra, Butterfield 8,* and *Ten North Frederick*—the final period adds two other novels, *Ourselves to Know* and *The Lockwood Concern,* as well as two minor, unpretentious novels that reveal an interest in sensibility, *Elizabeth Appleton* and *The Ewings.* An interest in sensibility and in his characters' inner psychological states distinguishes O'Hara's best work of this period, but O'Hara's themes are surprisingly consistent—as they are, in fact, throughout his career. In each of his phases as a novelist, the settings, characters, and narrative methods are varied, but the underlying vision is always the same one of isolation and loneliness.

So many rehearsals of the same theme suggest at least one of O'Hara's limitations as a novelist. Although resourceful in varying the narrative strategies of his novels and possessing impressive skills as a technician, O'Hara does not give the impression of having a large range of thematic ideas. He did not progress from early attitudes toward man and society to later ones farther along in his career, or develop wholly new preoccupations as time went on, as is the case with many other writers. His development from the early novels—taut, dramatic, and symbolically plotted—to the sprawling, allegorical family sagas, to the psychologically oriented last novels, was largely aesthetic. It has sometimes been said that O'Hara's particular interest is that he was a "social historian," but the pattern of his work, viewed more broadly, reveals him as an aesthetic analyst of an obsessive, prismatic theme.

8

Conclusion

In the previous chapters, O'Hara's own psychological patterns have been noted from time to time in their relation to the conflicts involved in his fictional conceptions. The relation between O'Hara's psychic stresses and compulsive preoccupations and the nature of the fiction he wrote is worth examining again at the end, since it is relevant to the vision that emerges in his work. In considering the sense one has of trauma and inner conflict in O'Hara, a good place to begin is his first major short story, "The Doctor's Son," a partly autobiographical tale in which Gibbsville is first introduced. In "The Doctor's Son," Dr. Malloy, based on O'Hara's father, occupies an important place in the minutely stratified life of the town, and could be said—as a town elder and father figure—to represent authority. At the opening of the story, however, as a virulent influenza epidemic devastates nearby Collieryville, Dr. Malloy's authority has begun to break down. Dr. Malloy needs rest and cannot go on, and a replacement for him is sent in the person of young "Dr." Myers, a medical student from Philadelphia. This intruder into the regulated life of the community brings confusion with him, and at the end "normal" relationships are shattered.

What Dr. Myers brings with him, specifically, is sexuality. He makes love to a married woman, a grave breach of professional ethics, and it is the more disturb-

ing because he is Dr. Malloy's own surrogate. It is as if
he represents an aspect of Dr. Malloy previously unsus-
pected by his adolescent son James. The story, however, could be read in another way that would also
have sexual implications, and would be perhaps even
more persuasive. Dr. Myers could be seen not only as
Dr. Malloy's deputy but also as a trusted son who betrays him. That Dr. Myers should sneakingly make love
to a woman who is also a *mother* has Oedipal implications too glaring to be missed when the reader considers
the antagonism and power struggle that exist between
Dr. Malloy and James. Sex, in any case, is the intruder
that cancels out any possibility of fulfilling human relationships or of love. It is associated distinctly with betrayal and death. The Evanses are destroyed as a family, but the story's focal sufferer is really James Malloy,
O'Hara's fictional *persona,* who loses the safety and
protection of a "family" and is thrust out into a terrible
world. The components of O'Hara's earliest traumas
all seem implied in "The Doctor's Son"—the conflict
between authority and rebellion, the introduction of
an unpermitted sexuality and self-assertion followed
by disorder, guilt, and severe punishment.

In *Appointment in Samarra,* written soon after
"The Doctor's Son," the same elements appear and are
in some respects clarified. Another father-son conflict
can be noted—in this case between Dr. English and his
son Julian, who suffers from feelings of inferiority and
unworthiness. The deepest truth about Julian, beneath
his sociability, is his *fear.* Dr. English's withholding of
his approval of Julian does not need to be expressed
directly; it is implicit in O'Hara's depiction of his cold
self-sufficiency, which makes him unable to understand Julian's need for his love. The fear in Julian is
that no òne loves him at all, neither his father nor
anyone else. His fear is felt most acutely in his relationship with his wife Caroline, whose preference for him

over other men he cannot quite "trust" because, at the deepest level of his consciousness, he does not believe it is deserved. He drinks to anesthetize himself, and finally climbs into his Cadillac to die of asphyxiation rather than face the terror of his isolation. Julian's life is especially doom-ridden through O'Hara's having invested his society with such an overwhelming sense of corruption that it seems a "fallen" world, a scene of damnation. Having "sinned," having failed the father to whom he feels answerable, Julian experiences the "warranted" punishment of an isolation so terrible that he can no longer go on living.

The sense of psychic crisis and doom in *Appointment in Samarra* is less acute in *Butterfield 8*, but the novel nevertheless reveals O'Hara's sexual fixation. New York society during the era of the Prohibition speakeasy is not only corrupt, but even viciously corrupt; and the novel's principal character is martyred to it. Gloria Wandrous is betrayed by men specifically and then by her society generally, and dies conspicuously alone. At the opening of *Butterfield 8*, Gloria is shown consumed with guilt that has followed in the wake of her sexual awakening, and she is eventually punished by a horrible death, whether or not the guilt she feels is deserved. In *Hope of Heaven*, James Malloy, now a Hollywood writer who has sold out his integrity in order to make money, is also pursued by guilt. Although he takes pleasure in his expensive clothes and the large house he is able to rent in Beverly Hills, he knows that he is "corrupt." Although Malloy does not die, the naive Keith who is unwilling to see what he does not want to, is put to death, after which Malloy recognizes that he is condemned to live out the empty life he has made for himself.

The Christmas episode in *Hope of Heaven* underscores the idea of profanation, and punishment follows in the final scene, from which the novel derives its title, where Malloy and Peggy Henderson discuss the Catholic conception of heaven, lost to both of them but particularly to Malloy. O'Hara's sexual theme is less conspicuous in *Hope of Heaven* than it is in *Butterfield 8*, but it is insinuated throughout. A womanizer, Malloy sleeps with a Los Angeles whore; but sexuality also lurks behind the facade of the other male characters, particularly Philip Henderson, who is soaked in materialism and is a chronic seducer of women, and Don Miller, who is accompanied in one scene by a whore (and is obliquely intimated to be homosexual as well). The people in Hollywood wear disguises, pretending to be respectable while they are actually devoid of innocence. James Malloy is entrapped in his isolation at the end because there is nothing in American society, as he knows it, that he can "trust." His attitude suggests a man who has either been or is about to be betrayed.

The motifs in O'Hara's novels of the thirties—sex, guilt, betrayal, and punishment—do not appear prominently in his early short stories; but the stories nevertheless testify to the squalid and corrupt nature of the world. In them, O'Hara writes with an attitude of defensiveness and a sense of hostility toward society and its members; and his overriding preoccupation is with maiming and frustration. More revealing are the novels that O'Hara next writes. In terms of bulk, *A Rage to Live* could hardly be more unlike O'Hara's spare novels of the thirties. But in this work, too, one notes O'Hara's repertoire of fixations. Essentially, *A Rage to Live* deals with an expulsion from innocence, the loss of former sureties symbolized by the Caldwell farm. With the death of his father, O'Hara was himself expelled into a frightening world, and he gives the impression that he never ceased to grieve over the injury inflicted upon his sense of identity. In *A Rage to Live*, O'Hara has specifically associated the loss of the home with an awakening to sexuality, which cannot lead to fulfilling human relationships. Sexuality is frequently evoked in the novel, in fact, in terms of internecine class warfare. At the opening of *A Rage to Live*, sex is something like the worm in the bud; in the end, the bud has bloomed into a cankered maturity that leaves everyone isolated from everyone else.

A charge sometimes made against O'Hara is that he was naively infatuated with sex, and littered his novels with it. Sex was clearly a major preoccupation with O'Hara, but it enters his novels as more than a prurient fascination and is, in fact, closely related to all the misery and isolation his characters suffer. Gore Vidal has protested that O'Hara's sex scenes are utterly joyless, without perceiving that they were meant to be. Grace Tate has sex with Roger Banon in the seat of an automobile with mechanical lust, and the effect their lovemaking produces is unpleasant and grotesque. Sex never leads to any enlargement in Grace's life, but, quite the reverse, dooms her to live in an unending exile. Sex in O'Hara's novels often has a "sinful" aspect (*A Rage to Live* deals literally with a fall from "grace") and is associated with disintegration and personal failure.

In *Ten North Frederick*, the chain of events that leads to Joe Chapin's isolation begins with the mother's refusal of sex, which injures her husband and then ultimately her son. In this novel, sex is associated positively with life—and yet in a way that is rather treacherous, since it cannot easily be coped with and, misused, may result in appalling damage. In *From the Terrace*, Natalie Benziger is evoked in terms of a sexuality that is related to a capacity to love, but she is virtually alone in having such associations. A vast number of other characters reveal a sexuality that seems diseased. Mary St. John Eaton, in her sexual nature, is one of the most unattractive characters in O'Hara's fiction, but there are many other versions of her in the work. Jim Roper and Sage

Remington have common cause with her. Other characters, like Percy Hasbrouck, display a cold malice that
is related to their incapacity for sex, and still others,
like Larry Von Elm, use sex meanly and vindictively as
a weapon of class warfare. One of the chief impressions
From the Terrace gives is that sex is unlovely and
malignant.

O'Hara's vision of a sexually menaced world is especially relevant to his male protagonists, since it strikes
at their sense of their masculinity. Julian English is an
early sufferer. His sense of his masculinity has been a
means by which he has attempted to ward off the threat
of life; but when at the end it comes to him that his
masculinity has been impaired and will not protect
him from the absolute helplessness he feels, he commits
suicide. Rather than being an anomaly in O'Hara's fiction, Julian reveals a pattern that appears repeatedly in
the later novels. Sidney Tate cannot stand up to his wife
Grace when he is confronted by her infidelity. He is
revealed at this point as a man who feels weak and de-
fenseless, who cowers before obscure inner terrors.
Had Sidney not died of polio, the reader could have
imagined no future for him. What gives *Ten North
Frederick* much of its tension is the threat of castration
that is posed and is, in fact, carried out in the course of
the novel. Not merely one but two women are involved, so that the threat of women is made to seem
actually conspiratorial. That Alfred Eaton, in *From the
Terrace*, is threatened in the same way by his wife,
Mary St. John, and is at the end helpless and emotionally impotent, adds to an impression of threat through
sexual intimacy in O'Hara's novels.

The phobic themes and recurrent patterns of fixation in the characters of his novels ultimately suggest a
paranoid tendency in O'Hara's own psychology, an
abnormally sensitive consciousness of external forces
that threaten his integrity or ability to function. It

comes out in his attitude of hostility and suspiciousness, the sense he gives that if he relaxes his defenses, allowing life to touch him too closely, he will be destroyed. It is implied in his tendency to harbor grudges against a world that has wronged and maimed him; and it is hinted at in the isolation he feels from others, but from which he cannot free himself. The idea of betrayal by society keeps entering his novels, and it is felt as being especially acute when it is connected with sex, which is often projected as being menacing, sometimes triggering actual terror in his male characters.

Interestingly, in his final period as a novelist, O'Hara reexamines his persistent theme of a tense self-enclosure and isolation in terms of neuroticism. Robert Millhouser in *Ourselves to Know*, for example, is less a victim of society than of his own nature. What the exact source of his frustration is remains unclear at the end, but it is felt most strongly on the level of sexual fear. His wife Hedda represents one of the most aggressively unpleasant versions of female sexuality in all O'Hara's writing—which is saying much; and it is with Hedda most of all that Millhouser cannot come to terms.[1] In other novels of the period—in *The Big Laugh, The Instrument,* and *Lovey Childs*—sexuality is implied to be loathsome; and *The Instrument,* in addition, envisions life as being essentially cannibalistic in nature. Yank Lucas, in *The Instrument,* is an embittered grudge holder who cannot forget or forgive his failed relationship with his father or the infidelity of his wife. Emotionally maimed, he is abnormally conscious of the aggressive designs of the other characters; and although he has a brief sexual relationship with Zena Gollum, he soon withdraws into his cerebral work, "loving" Zena in a work of art that he controls and manipulates.

In *The Lockwood Concern,* George Lockwood is more solipsistic even than Robert Millhouser, and is more neurotically alone. He is given an elaborate family background to account for his fixation, his "mania." But more specifically, with his isolated house, tall, spiked wall surrounding it, and secret staircase, he gives the sense of the paranoid imagination come into full flower. He trusts no one because, in paranoid fashion, he projects upon them the aggressive impulses that he harbors within himself; and closed away in his secretiveness, he nurtures grandiose ambitions and schemes. Lockwood is not, however, entirely as singular as he at first seems, since he reflects on other characters of O'Hara's late period—on Millhouser, who builds a spider's web of introspection around him to keep the world at a distance, and Yank Lucas, who recognizes that the world is menaced by emotional aggressors.

The sense of trauma in O'Hara, of deep, unresolved conflict, affects his novels in many ways, providing a tremendous charge of intensity in many of his characters' situations, but also at times creating a sense of the loathsomeness of life in excess of what the reader can accept. But if O'Hara's psychological patterns sometimes bear closely on his fiction, they do not explain it entirely or account for his achievement. O'Hara's achievement in the short story still goes unchallenged, even by critics who have reservations about his work as a novelist. O'Hara was the preeminent short story writer of his time in America, producing a large body of work of significant stature. O'Hara's early stories depict a dark and enigmatic world in which the irrational waits to break out at any time. Characters sometimes make horrible recognitions about the emptiness of their lives, but those who do not seem equally condemned, in their failure of self-knowledge. Many versions of claustrophobia or emotional scarring are encountered, but each is distinct, brought to life immediately, and rendered, as one critic has remarked, with "the photographic precision of the still-life painter." And although social experience in the stories is rendered with a strictly linear effect, the reader is also, remarkably, made conscious of depths beneath surfaces, of aching voids of loneliness in the characters' lives.

The later stories tend not only to be much longer than the early ones but also introduce new modulations of tone, manner, and attitude. Character portraiture is more fully rendered, with a new emphasis upon sensibility, and sometimes with a more generous attitude toward the characters. O'Hara at times becomes an elegist, able to extend compassion to his characters because they are now perceived as sharing in "the common doom." Most of all, what may be noted in these tales is a new elegance, an emphasis upon nuances of psychology and the variegated textures of social experience. These stories suggest the subtlety and control of form of a polished observer of manners.

The perfection of O'Hara's short stories raises the question, however, of the imperfection of O'Hara's novels, of why it is that O'Hara's mastery of the shorter form did not carry over into the longer. Oddly, O'Hara's masterpiece, *Appointment in Samarra*, was also the first novel he wrote. The other novels can be faulted in one respect or another, in certain cases gravely. One problem for O'Hara as a novelist is the two-dimensionality of his characters. His two-dimensional characters fill out his short stories, which focus upon a single incident or scene; but they do not always expand to meet the requirements of the novel. Grace Tate is an example of a character who lacks the inner dimensionality called for in a work of considerable length. *A Rage to Live* has to expand around her, with the result that it is prolonged for hundreds of pages of seemingly superfluous social observation. *From the Terrace* suffers from the same problem. Alfred Eaton is a generic "type," incapable of sustaining a depth of interest for nine hundred pages.

In *Appointment in Samarra* and *Butterfield 8*,

O'Hara's characters have fixed natures and limited fields of awareness, but a concise dramatic structure has been provided for their interaction, so that they seem to live to the extent of their possibilities. The longer social chronicles, however, lack the economy and intensity of these structures. In *Ten North Frederick*, even though it is one of O'Hara's better novels, Joe Chapin cannot fill the frame that is provided for him; the reader cannot enter into his interior life because he has none. O'Hara is therefore compelled to build his drama at the suggestive outer edges rather than at the center of Joe Chapin's experience. One of the satisfactions the novel normally yields is that its characters change or develop in the course of their experience, but O'Hara's characters have fixed identities that do not permit such inner expansion. Robert Millhouser is presented with elaborate narrative complexity, but his nature is always determined and he can only ponder why this should be so. George Lockwood is not free to be other than fixated in the precise mental pattern that he reveals; he seems to have been born the way he is and can never be otherwise.

It might also be noted that many of the strategies O'Hara uses in attempting to compensate for the static conception of his characters belong to the short story form. The episodic nature of O'Hara's family chronicles, for example, allows him to shape the works in an expanding sequence of vignettes that are like concise short stories within the novel; the scene in *Ten North Frederick* where Edith Chapin is suddenly visited by a lesbian friend from college is perfectly self-contained and could stand by itself as a strikingly executed vignette-like story. O'Hara also introduces a large number of subordinate characters who come to life quickly, like short story characters, and are not expected to have complicated interiors. His use of irony in the endings of the novels, as in *A Rage to Live*, is reminiscent of the ironic endings of his short fiction;

and the ending of *The Ewings,* with its focal shift to the gnawing loneliness of Clarence Kelley's life, is typical of one of O'Hara's favorite short story devices—the postponed revelation.

That a number of the weaknesses in O'Hara's novels have no parallel in his short stories confirms an impression that the novel form produced a strain on O'Hara's creative imagination. The implausible motivation O'Hara sometimes gives to major characters; his introduction of subordinate characters who have no clear part to play and drop out of the narratives; the wandering quality of some of the writing, and O'Hara's prolixity—none of these things would have been tolerated in his short stories. As a novelist, O'Hara wrote at times too hastily, or at least too uncritically, and he gave too much importance to what he called "the hefting test" of a novel, as if the number of pages of a novel by itself constituted strength. Throughout his career, O'Hara gave the impression of searching for his "form" in the novel without, at the end, having quite found it.

But he ought to be allowed his virtues. At his best, O'Hara could be very good indeed. Even after forty years, *Appointment in Samarra* still seems as fresh as when it was first written. In each of his phases as a novelist, O'Hara produced work of superior quality that enters into the mood of its period. *Ten North Frederick,* with its theme of conventional success that conceals the agony of inner defeat, captures the sense of the fifties as much as any of Marquand's novels; and *Ourselves to Know* and *The Lockwood Concern,* with their envisioning of psychological alienation, belong to the concern with the irrationality of the sixties. In a technical sense, O'Hara was remarkably versatile, shifting his narrative method from novel to novel, and achieving at times impressive effects, as in the brilliantly sustained, hundred-page opening "scene" in *Ten North Frederick.* The complicated movement back and forth in time and the medley of narrative voices in *Ourselves to Know* reflect O'Hara's lifelong experimentation with narrative form; and the narrative structure of *From the Terrace,* in which Alfred Eaton's career is projected against the simultaneous growth to power and impotence of America, is an achievement on the order of Dos Passos's *U.S.A.* trilogy.

O'Hara is also distinguished through his having created his own "region," as Sherwood Anderson had created Winesburg and the surrounding landscapes of Ohio and the Midwest, and as Faulkner had created Yoknapatawpha County. As a creator of a fictional region, O'Hara perhaps most closely resembles the English Arnold Bennett in the literalness of his realism—although romantic energies are sometimes concealed beneath his literalism, as they are not in the case of Bennett. If the short stories set in or near Lantenengo County are taken together with the novels, O'Hara would have to be credited with establishing a region of some density. It is created with a plenitude and fullness on every social level, from the lowest to the highest; and any discussion of the modern American novelist's concern with a region would have to take O'Hara's fiction into account.

O'Hara was not a philosophical writer, like Melville, who asked eternal questions about man and the universe. His mind had a smaller calibration, and was equipped best to deal with what was practical and near at hand. His handicap was part of his strength, for he was able to "see" certain aspects of American life with enormous concentrativeness. Few novelists can compare with O'Hara in his ability to create vivid social surfaces with expertness and detachment, and no one at all can compare with his ear for American speech. His gift as a mimic of voices and social types was prodigious. Like some comic Irishman with a lethal gift for taking off his neighbors, he was able to impersonate everyone, from the scullery maids in *Ourselves to Know* to the fine lady abovestairs.

The scullery maids in *Ourselves to Know* are a

good example of O'Hara's ability to come to the point
instantly in his characterizations. One of them, a Mrs.
Daub, is "a good cook and an excellent pastry chef, a fat
woman who was often to be found sitting at a kitchen
table with her eyes open and yet apparently sound
asleep, with a half-eaten piece of cake and a cup of tea
getting cold before her." Mrs. Daub is visualized distinctly and immediately, but O'Hara can as quickly capture the corporate executive or Wall Street financier,
the Irish policeman, the harlot, the Jewish movie producer, the self-made mayor of a small town, the bartender and his barber, the North Shore socialite, the
suburban housewife, the law firm senior partner, the
upper middle class matron who examines her hands to
see if they are "efficient." With a formidable gift for
visualization, O'Hara creates a vast gallery of characters of almost every conceivable type.

As a chronicler of materialistic middle-class life in
America, O'Hara has sometimes been compared to
Sinclair Lewis, an indebtedness O'Hara himself acknowledged. It is extraordinary how seriously both
Lewis and O'Hara take the American town, down to
the minutest manifestations of its life, how accurately
they place their characters within local hierarchies.
They are both mimics of distinctively American types,
and give unusual importance to their peculiar speech.
But the resemblance between them pertains only to a
certain portion of O'Hara's writing, and even in this
case O'Hara seems the more modern. Similarities also
exist, in certain respects, between O'Hara and John Dos
Passos, both of whom experimented with the pattern
or mosaic novel, and were fascinated by grotesqueness
in their characters' lives, by their abortive careers and
misshapen destinies. Dos Passos's Margot Dowling in
the *U.S.A.* trilogy is the crowning type of O'Hara's vacant movie queens, and his Charley Anderson, the
American entrepreneur who finally goes bankrupt,
would have fit in well in *From the Terrace*. Dos Passos
and O'Hara both work with two-dimensional charac-

ters, playing off their lives with the growth into monstrous incoherence and fragmentation of contemporary American civilization.

But the father figure to O'Hara is F. Scott Fitzgerald. It was very fitting that O'Hara's career as a novelist should have begun with Fitzgerald's reading the manuscript of *Appointment in Samarra* while, at the same time, O'Hara read the galley proofs of *Tender Is the Night*. It is as if a bond between them had been formalized. Like Fitzgerald, O'Hara came out of an Irish Catholic background and could imagine only frustration and defeat for the heroes of his novels. Fitzgerald writes of the failure of love in the context of the American dream, and the failure of love is always at the center of O'Hara's, often in the context of an American civilization that cannot provide a basis for communication between people. Curiously, the infidelity-betrayal theme that is so prominent in O'Hara's novels can also be seen in Fitzgerald's. *The Great Gatsby* is concerned centrally with Gatsby's "guilty" affair with Daisy Fay Buchanan, and ends with his death when he is betrayed by her; and in *Tender Is the Night*, Dick Diver is betrayed and even unmanned by Nicole Warren, whom he marries. Fitzgerald's heroes, with noble natures, are plunged into a darkly romantic isolation by their tainting involvement with a corrupt world; and O'Hara's heroes suffer a naturalistic isolation in a world made corrupt by human nature and sexuality. The linked themes of sex-guilt and the punishment of a living perdition connect the work of these two Irish Catholic apostates.

Fitzgerald and O'Hara are also similar in their gravitation toward a socially oriented fiction, and shared interest in the life of the rich and well-to-do. According to one anecdote, when O'Hara occupied a terraced high-rise apartment on Sutton Place, he was supposed to have observed yachts on the East River through a pair of binoculars, checking the owners' names on the hulls against the Social Register. This well-known anecdote is no doubt apocryphal, but it is confirmed by all his biographers that O'Hara was fascinated by and studied the Social Register. He schooled himself in all the gradations of rank of preparatory schools, colleges, and private clubs and was alert to every insignia of social position. He became affluent himself, and took particular pleasure in associating with the rich. Fitzgerald's attitude toward the rich was ambivalent. He was attracted to an aesthetic style of life that wealth made possible, but his deepest attitude was one of the deepest hostility. Fitzgerald was a very sharp observer of the rich, but he suffered from one limitation. He did not enter very fully into their life, was a poor boy who looked on from some privileged outer edge of their world. In the end, he condemned the rich, who touched some inner chord of fear in him.

O'Hara mingled with the rich more fully than Fitzgerald, and he wrote about them as if he had an insider's view of them. But in O'Hara, too, a hostility toward the rich can be noted. This hostility took the form of his bringing them down to the commonest level. O'Hara's rich people—the Tates, for example—are as common in their sexual natures, as miserable in their lives, and as morally deficient as his lower-class characters. But by making the wealthy characters of his novels studies in primal, deterministic drives, O'Hara tended to bypass the whole field of "manners." If the fine lady and Judy O'Grady are the same under the skin, there is no need for "manners." In the end, O'Hara created a kind of mock version of the rich, a counterfeit version made to look authentic by knowing references, and was no more able to enter fully into their subtly "special" world than was Fitzgerald.

One of the primal emotions in Fitzgerald and O'Hara, after all, was the sense of exclusion. Fitzgerald's Amory Blaine in *This Side of Paradise* is reduced to humiliating, acute shock when he comes to recognize that he does not belong among the social "best," and, somewhat similarly, one critic has described O'Hara as "an Irishman who ate his heart out because he did not pass for society in the hard-coal region of Pennsylvania."[2] O'Hara was literally excluded from consideration as their daughter's suitor by a wealthy WASP family in Pottsville, very much as Amory Blaine was blacklisted by the wealthy family of Rosalind Connage. Fitzgerald and O'Hara had in common that they were both Irishmen who felt aggrieved and, as moralists, subscribed to a view of the world as black and treacherous. O'Hara's sense of a shared identity with Fitzgerald continued throughout his career. In his introduction to *The Portable F. Scott Fitzgerald* (1944), which helped to launch the Fitzgerald revival, O'Hara spent much of his space attacking Sinclair Lewis, with the implication that it is not at all to Lewis's tradition in American fiction that he, O'Hara, belongs but to Fitzgerald's.

In certain cases, O'Hara's fictional conceptions were affected by Fitzgerald's. *Appointment in Samarra* and *Butterfield 8* both reflect the influence of *The Great Gatsby;* and a number of O'Hara's short stories that involve nostalgia, both early and late, are strongly reminiscent of Fitzgerald. But whether in a nostalgic vein or not, it is loss, closed-off possibility, and defeat that tie O'Hara inseparably to Fitzgerald. If O'Hara had been more widely read, it is possible that Fitzgerald's influence might have been less. But he also served O'Hara well. He provided him with a model of sensibility and accomplished observation in social fiction, without which O'Hara's work would have been poorer indeed. An oddity of O'Hara's work is that part of it is dominated by a naturalistic literalism, while another part allies itself with a Fitzgeraldian love of nuance and subtlety. When these two aspects of his fiction come together, O'Hara's work has both firmness and sophistication.

O'Hara's critical reputation passed through two distinct phases. In the 1930s, he was widely regarded as one of the most promising of the younger American

writers. By the late 1950s, however, particularly with
the publication of *From the Terrace*, his reputation
declined, and has not recovered since. What happened
to O'Hara's reputation at the end of the fifties and in
the sixties can be explained partly by his having written a long series of best-selling novels of uneven quality, some of which show him at his worst. To many
conservative academic critics, O'Hara became tainted
by his popularity. His commercial success and endless
concern with the bedroom lives of his characters made
O'Hara seem to them a writer who need no longer be
taken seriously. Nor did he have the advantage of
being easily labeled; he was not quite a novelist of
manners, but on the other hand he was not wholly a
proletarian realist. Leftist critics attacked O'Hara particularly for his lack of political consciousness, his concern with surfaces and failure to probe beneath these
surfaces to confront the forces that shape the destiny
of society.

Other American social novelists also came under
attack in the late fifties and sixties; James Gould Cozzens, for example, was savaged by Dwight Macdonald,
in *Against the American Grain* (1963), as the quintes-
sential conservative and quietist writer of the Eisen-
hower period, the champion of the "Middlebrow
Counter-Revolution" against the supposed excesses of
the avant-garde intellectuals. He was virtually dismissed for writing the "Novel of Resignation," in which
"the highest reach of enlightenment is to realize how
awful the System is and yet to accept it *on its own
terms.*" But no writer of his stature was subjected to
such concerted dismissal in the 1960s as O'Hara. It became fashionable in *The New York Review of Books*
for critics to refer to O'Hara as a "middle-brow" or
bourgeois novelist uninterested in "the activity of the
mind." It was in this publication that Gore Vidal an-
nounced that "O'Hara's work cannot be taken seriously
as literature."[3] The intensity of the intellectually elitist
community's rejection of O'Hara gives the impression

that it was based on other than strictly aesthetic grounds. Alfred Kazin, for example, has written of O'Hara with unceasing hostility, but has never had difficulty in "forgiving" the more seriously flawed workmanship of Dreiser, who is, after all, acceptably "liberal," deals with working-class characters, and attacks the evils of American society.

In the shift in American literary taste and sensibility of the late fifties and sixties, O'Hara became the "enemy," an alienationist of the earlier generation who was no longer "relevant." He was not urban enough, or radical enough, or cerebral or modernistic enough. He was still absorbed by the American town, and took no interest in the intellectual ferment of New York. His sense of society was static and centrist; did not deal with alienated Jews or oppressed blacks, or marches on Washington where Dwight Macdonald and Norman Mailer locked hands to protest the dehumanization of the war in Vietnam. O'Hara was if anything hostile to liberals and protestors, writing with a pessimism that precluded the possibility of amelioration in American society. It is perhaps understandable, given their biases, that the taste makers of the sixties should have rejected O'Hara, but there is surely an intolerance in their having written him wholly out of literature. The acceptance of the social "given," or the status quo, affects not only O'Hara's writing but also much of social fiction itself, and particularly the novel of manners which, conservatively and reflectively, addresses itself to the conventional nature of life and to its characters' recognitions of themselves within the confines of these conventions. O'Hara's lack of political consciousness and acceptance of the "given" do not, in themselves, certify the valuelessness of his work.

Even today recognition of O'Hara in the universities is so slight that it is almost as if he had never entered into the development of American fiction from the 1930s through the 1960s. Sheldon Grebstein's concise, intelligent, surprisingly positive appraisal of almost twenty years ago is the only critical book published on O'Hara in the past, and very few essays on him exist at all. The neglect into which O'Hara has fallen can be gauged by the fact that his more than four hundred short stories, superb of their kind, have never been the subject of a book, a monograph, or even an essay of any length. As a result, many generalizations about O'Hara have not been examined. O'Hara once wrote in the introduction to one of his short story collections, for example, that the use of symbolism in fiction was over his head, something he knew nothing about; and since then a number of critics have noted that O'Hara almost always avoided any kind of symbolism in his writing—a statement that could hardly be less true. O'Hara's remark in the introduction was disingenuous, intended to mislead the unwary. The previous chapters on O'Hara's novels make it abundantly clear that he made use of symbolic devices elaborately, often with considerable sophistication.

Surprisingly for a writer whose work is sometimes crudely plotted or imperfectly realized, O'Hara's interest is to a large degree aesthetic. He is capable of very refined observation and great finesse in his handling of characters and their developing situations. His short stories reveal these qualities continually, but they appear in the novels too, and in one special quality he is approached by no one. Although his characters are characteristically two-dimensional, he creates a psychological atmosphere around them at times that is extraordinary. His ability to "sense" or "feel" a character within the context of an introspective mood can be seen in even his worst novels. Mildred Simmons and the party she gives, and Nina Stephens when she first appears, in *The Big Laugh*, have this special quality of being felt through a projected mood that is full of tones. The Eaton mother in her widowhood as she talks to her daughter-in-law in *From the Terrace* is captured with

the same psychological inwardness. This power of projection, usually witnessed in O'Hara's women, might be
called "depth of tone," and it is but one aspect of an
aesthetic richness in O'Hara that has been slighted or
ignored.

O'Hara cannot be called a major novelist, and his
achievement is not at the level of Hemingway, Fitzgerald, or Faulkner. But if his best work in fiction is
taken together—his short stories, nouvelles, and perhaps seven of his novels—he compares well with his
contemporaries: with John Steinbeck, John P. Marquand, James Gould Cozzens, James T. Farrell, and
John Hersey. Compared to Steinbeck, O'Hara produced a larger body of superior work, and his social
intelligence is almost infinitely more mature. O'Hara is
an elusive writer, but if he creates a tradition in American fiction, it is perhaps in the role he adopts as a musing observer of American middle-class despair. The
writers who follow him, in his special concerns, are
John Cheever and John Updike, who bring a similar
sense of disquiet and subterranean anguish to the suburbs. Their characters are portrayed in a closely specified social dimension, and yet are always subject to the
terrors that followed O'Hara—their isolation and entrapment within the abysses of themselves. O'Hara's career
began with trauma and psychic fixation, from which
he was unable to free himself; he could not write them
out of his system or evade them. From the fly-by-night
hotel rooms he occupied as a reporter to his "Linebrook" study outside Princeton, the terror of his loneliness was always part of him. But in his magical moments as a writer—and he has many—his haunting
becomes everyone's.

Notes

1. JOHN O'HARA: THE CONTOUR OF A LIFE

1. O'Hara began to correspond with F. Scott Fitzgerald in the early 1930s, and later spent time with him in January and February 1934, when Fitzgerald came to New York from Baltimore to see *Tender Is the Night* through publication. Fitzgerald read O'Hara's draft of *Appointment in Samarra* at this time, and O'Hara reciprocated by proofreading *Tender Is the Night*. When O'Hara completed his novel he wrote to thank Fitzgerald for reading and commenting on it. "You helped me finish my novel," he wrote. "I finished it yesterday. The little we talked when you were in New York did it. I reasoned that the best parts of my novel will be said to derive from Fitzgerald, and I think I have muffed my story, but I became reconciled to having done that after talking to you and reading *Tender Is the Night* in proof. No one else can write like that, and I haven't tried, but the best parts of my novel are facile pupils of *The Beautiful and Damned* and *The Great Gatsby*." Quoted in Matthew J. Bruccoli, *The O'Hara Concern: A Biography of John O'Hara* (New York: Random House, 1975), p. 101. Although not found among his papers, the proofs of *Tender Is the Night* were said by O'Hara to be among his most precious possessions; and a copy of the novel, inscribed to him by Fitzgerald, was in O'Hara's bedroom when he died.

    O'Hara saw Fitzgerald again in Hollywood in 1937 and 1939, and the two were photographed together. In

1945, O'Hara wrote the introduction to *The Portable F. Scott Fitzgerald,* which played a part in launching the Fitzgerald revival. In the introduction he remarked: "All [Fitzgerald] was was our best novelist, one of our best novella-ists, and one of our finest writers of short stories." In 1949, in a letter to John Steinbeck, referring to American writers since the First World War, O'Hara commented that "Fitzgerald was a just plain better writer than all of us put together." (John O'Hara, *Selected Letters of John O'Hara,* edited by Matthew J. Bruccoli [New York: Random House, 1978], p. 224.) In a July 30, 1962, letter to Gerald Murphy, who had been the model, in part, for Dick Diver in *Tender Is the Night,* O'Hara commented again on Fitzgerald in the same vein. "Sooner or later," he wrote, "his characters always came back to being Fitzgerald characters in a Fitzgerald world. He was really quite shocked by *Butterfield 8,* because no matter what his own conduct was, it did not seem to belong in a Fitzgerald world. He was our best novelist in spite of this limitation." (*Selected Letters of John O'Hara,* p. 402.)

2.   Quoted in Frank MacShane, *The Life of John O'Hara* (New York: E. P. Dutton, 1980), p. 107.

3.   O'HARA THE NOVELIST: FIRST FLIGHT— *Appointment in Samarra*

1.   John O'Hara, *Selected Letters of John O'Hara,* p. 402. Letter to Gerald Murphy, July 30, 1962.

2.   *Appointment in Samarra* is especially striking in its filmlike visualization of its material. O'Hara had not worked as a screenwriter at the time of its composition, but he had been employed in New York as a publicity agent for a Hollywood studio and had reviewed films for various publications. A similar use of montagelike effects and film technique is especially strong in Fitzgerald's *Tender Is the Night;* but since O'Hara had completed most of his novel before reading the galley proofs of *Tender,* it would be difficult to see how this

novel could have influenced his own. A more likely influence is *The Great Gatsby*, in which the various chapters have a distinct unity but are composed of fragmented scenes, involving sudden, dramatic "camera-cut"
transitions.

3. In his forword to the publication of *Appointment in
    Samarra* in the Modern Library edition, O'Hara re-
    marked: "In the matter of influences, here they are:
    Fitzgerald, Sinclair Lewis, Galsworthy, Tarkington,
    Owen Johnson, but chiefly Fitzgerald and Lewis. If
    Hemingway influenced me the influence is not appar-
    ent to me, and I *can* see countless instances of the effect
    of my reading Fitzgerald and Lewis." John O'Hara,
    Appointment in Samarra (New York: Modern Library,
    1953), p. iv.

4. *Appointment in Samarra* resembles *The Great Gatsby*
    in a number of specific respects—the sense of "corrup-
    tion" in the society O'Hara depicts, for example, and
    the manner in which the hero is singled out to pay the
    penalty for his involvement in this corrupt world. As in
    The Great Gatsby, the corruption of the society in *Ap-
    pointment in Samarra* is underscored through Christian
    and mythological associations. The Christ idea is evi-
    dent through O'Hara's having set the novel during the
    three days of Julian's suffering; and Julian's name may
    also suggest Julian the Apostate of Scripture. The
    sleazy Apollo restaurant where Al Grecco has his
    Christmas meal debases the implication of elevated
    vision suggested by the Greek god in a way that is sim-
    ilar to Fitzgerald's use of the Apollo myth in his novel.
    The Apollo restaurant scene, moreover, a setting in
    which ideals have been abandoned, is reminiscent spe-
    cifically of the Greek restaurant in the Valley of Ashes,
    a godforsaken building approached by a trail of ashes.
    In both novels, a close link is established between sexu-
    ality and death; and at the end of *Appointment in
    Samarra*, Julian is "sacrificed"—dying alone, as Gatsby
    dies alone.

5. O'Hara acknowledged Hemingway's influence on his
    early stories, and Edmund Wilson has commented on

the two in the following way: "John O'Hara also derives from Hemingway, and his short stories sound superficially like Hemingway's. . . . But O'Hara's main interest in life is of an entirely different category of fiction. O'Hara is not a poet like Hemingway, but primarily a social commentator; and in this field of social habits and manners . . . he has done work that is original and interesting." Edmund Wilson, *Classics and Commercials* (New York: Farrar, Straus & Giroux, 1950), p. 22.

6. *Ibid.*, p. 23.

7. Lionel Trilling, Introduction, *Selected Short Stories of John O'Hara* (New York: Modern Library, 1956), p. x.

8. Arthur Mizener, Afterword, *Appointment in Samarra* (New York: New American Library Signet, 1963), pp. 207–15. Mizener remarks that O'Hara's "marvelous imaginative grasp of what it feels like for each social group to live in Gibbsville is the real subject of the book; the story of Julian English merely provides plot." O'Hara was angered by Mizener's "Afterword," as he should have been, since it robs the novel of any intrinsic aesthetic complexity or interest.

4. *Butterfield 8* and *Hope of Heaven:* COMPLETING THE TRILOGY OF THE THIRTIES

1. Percy Kahan, as a Jewish parvenu, seems indebted to Fitzgerald's conception of Joseph Bloeckman in *The Beautiful and Damned,* just as he, in turn, seems inspired by Simon Rosedale in Edith Wharton's *The House of Mirth.*

2. O'Hara's first Hollywood assignment, writing additional dialogue for films, came in 1934 and was followed by similar assignments in 1936–1937 and 1939. In the 1940s and 1950s, he contributed to films sporadically, usually revising the dialogue of other writers' scripts. Five of his books were made into films—*Pal Joey* (1957), *Ten North Frederick* (1958), *Butterfield 8* (1960), *From the Terrace* (1960), and *A Rage to Live*

(1965)—but O'Hara had no part in their adaption for the screen. For a detailed chronology of O'Hara's work for Hollywood, see Bruccoli, *The O'Hara Concern*, p. 286.

3. O'Hara's adaptation of *Pal Joey* as a musical play, presented on Broadway in 1940, was his most notable achievement in writing for the stage. Between 1940 and 1970, he worked on at least sixteen other plays, to some degree or other, but relatively few were completed, and none was presented on Broadway. For details of these projects, see Bruccoli, p. 210. In later years, O'Hara seems to have discounted the chance of his plays' being produced, and worked on them for brief periods to distract himself while he waited for reviews of his novels to appear. O'Hara's published plays are *The Farmers Hotel, The Searching Sun, The Champagne Pool, Veronique,* and *The Way It Was,* all in John O'Hara, *Five Plays* (New York: Random House, 1961), and *Far from Heaven,* in *Two by O'Hara* (New York: Harcourt Brace Jovanovich, 1979). The plays are generally too modest to require comment. The most accomplished of them is *The Farmers Hotel,* written in 1946–1947 and presented on network television in 1952; his most psychologically interesting play is *Far from Heaven,* a sinister mood study of a character's disintegrating identity.

4. In addition to his roles in *Butterfield 8* and *Hope of Heaven,* James Malloy is the narrator of the three nouvelles in *Sermons and Soda-Water* and appears, in a few cases without being identified by name, in the following stories: "The Doctor's Son," "It Must Have Been Spring," and "Dr. Wyeth's Son" (*The Doctor's Son*); "Pardner," "Transaction," "Miss W.," and "Conversation in the Atomic Age" (*Hellbox*); "The Man with the Broken Arm" and "In the Silence" (*Assembly*); "Exterior with Figures" (*The Hat on the Bed*); "Fatima and Kisses" (*Waiting for Winter*); "A Few Trips and Some Poetry" (*And Other Stories*); "A Man to be Trusted," "The Journey to Mount Clemens," and "The Mechanical Man" (*Good Samaritan*).

5. THE FAMILY SAGA NOVELS OF THE MIDDLE PERIOD: *A Rage to Live*, *Ten North Frederick*, and *From the Terrace*

1. F. Scott Fitzgerald, *The Letters of F. Scott Fitzgerald*, p. 539. Letter to John O'Hara, July 25, 1936.
2. Quoted in Frank MacShane, *The Life of John O'Hara*, p. 140.
3. *The Farmers Hotel* (1951), a one-hundred-and-fifty-three page nouvelle, is a novelized version of O'Hara's play of the same title written five years earlier, and its three parts correspond to the three acts of a play. It is set in rural Pennsylvania at an inn, or farmers hotel, on the first day and night of its opening. As a late November snowstorm develops, a number of strangers appear at the inn, come to know one another briefly and, for a time, enter into a spirit of comradeship. The mood is then broken by one of the guests, a bully named Joe Rogg, who is expelled from the inn, and later vindictively, drives his diesel rig into the car of two of the departing guests, killing them instantly. O'Hara's sureness of handling is seen in his subtle creation of mood, ease of movement from one set of characters to another, and insinuation of development although hardly anything seems to be happening. The sudden violence of the ending seems strained, but *The Farmers Hotel* is otherwise an impressively controlled piece of writing.
4. *A Family Party* (1956) is set in the Pennsylvania town of Lyons, and is narrated in the form of a monologue. The occasion of the story is a testimonial dinner given in honor of Dr. Sam Merritt, retiring after forty years of practice in the community. The speaker is his old friend Albert Shoemaker, formerly editor of the local newspaper, the Lyons *Republican*. What makes the story immediately engaging is the authority of the narrator's voice, which influences the reader to feel that he knows him intimately. Shoemaker is "American small town" in all his intonations, his assumption of fellowship with his audience. In eulogizing his friend, the narrator indulges

in fond personal reminiscences, tells anecdotes and little stories, reminds himself that he is digressing. For the
first half or more of A Family Party, the reader has the
sense that the story is very charming in itself but perhaps has no great point. Then late in the account come
the postponed revelations of tragedy in Merritt's life—
his wife's miscarriages and her mental breakdown. It is
in her name that people in Lyons have raised funds to
establish a ward in a nearby hospital. Reviewers described A Family Party as "warm-hearted" and "mel-
low," if slightly sentimental, failing to recognize it as
one of O'Hara's cruelly ironic monologues.

Although an admirable man, deserving of his fellow citizens' commendation, Sam Merritt becomes, by
the end, a painful study in failure. In an incident that is
mentioned in passing and might easily be overlooked, it
is brought out that Dr. Merritt has raised funds, including $30,000 from his close relatives, to build a hospital
in Lyons. Another doctor, however, hearing of the un-
dertaking, gained support of an influential bank and
put through his own plan to build a hospital in nearby
Johnsville. Finding his project preempted, Merritt then
turned over the funds he had raised to the hospital
sponsored by the other doctor—a generous act, no
doubt, but surely an awkward and humiliating experience for him.

But Merritt's failure implied in this incident is nothing compared to his marriage. After having two miscarriages, his wife sank into depression, and was sent to a
private hospital in Fort Penn. At the time of the testimonial dinner, she has been a mental patient for twenty-
five years, her case considered incurable. The narrator
speaks tenderly and respectfully of Dr. Merritt and his
beloved wife, but the more he reveals the more grotesque the doctor's life seems. There is a terrible irony
surely in the fact that citizens of Lyons have raised
funds for a maternity ward to be named for Dr. Merritt's wife, who was unable to bear children! The title of
the work, a "family" party, is also revealing, since Dr.
Merritt's family has consisted, gruesomely, of stillborn

children and an absent, insane wife. What the narrator of *A Family Party* unwillingly reveals is that the honored guest's life has been lonely and anguished.

5. O'Hara's observation of men in public life inspired several of his novels. His conception of Joe Chapin in *Ten North Frederick* was suggested by Franklin Roosevelt, his dominating and matriarchal mother Sara, and his wife Eleanor. Ironically, Chapin, who has a secret ambition to become president of the United States, is a kind of Roosevelt without his capacities.

7. The Late Novels: The Spectrum from *Ourselves to Know* to *The Ewings*

1. *The Second Ewings* (Columbia, South Carolina: Bruccoli Clark, 1977) is a seventy-four-page fragment published posthumously in a limited edition of five hundred copies, and available chiefly at research libraries. Prompted in part by *The Forsyte Saga* television series of the late 1960s, *The Second Ewings* begins when Bill Ewing is thirty-five and chairman of the Cuyahoga board. From the fragment, however, it is difficult to tell what the novel might have dealt with. A facsimile of O'Hara's yellow copy-paper typescript, with his corrections written in pen, it gives the reader an almost eerie sense of looking over O'Hara's shoulder as he worked at his typewriter in his "Linebrook" study.

2. O'Hara's nonfiction collections, which are very slight, include *Sweet and Sour* (New York: Random House, 1954); *My Turn* (New York: Random House, 1966); and *"An Artist Is His Own Fault": John O'Hara on Writers and Writing*, edited by Matthew J. Bruccoli (Carbondale: Southern Illinois University Press, 1977). *Sweet and Sour* consists of journalistic pieces O'Hara wrote for the Trenton *Times-Advertiser*, and *My Turn* collects fifty-two columns of opinion O'Hara wrote for *Newsday*. In *My Turn*, O'Hara expresses a variety of personal opinions in a truculent manner, from his defense of cigarette smoking to his hostile views of Martin

Luther King and liberal politicians. Sheldon Grebstein has characterized the volume well in remarking that in reading it one waits with "dreadful anticipation of O'Hara's next blunder." *"An Artist Is His Own Fault"* is a slender volume containing some of O'Hara's speeches, reviews, and literary articles, particularly his three lectures on writing at Rider College, delivered in 1959 and 1961. The Rider College lectures are of interest inasmuch as they show O'Hara defending himself from the critical view of him as a "social historian" rather than a literary artist. The title, "An Artist Is His Own Fault," was used by O'Hara in connection with F. Scott Fitzgerald.

8. CONCLUSION

1. O'Hara's female castrators also raise the question of latent or repressed homosexuality in O'Hara. The patterns of O'Hara's psychology, as has been noted, suggest a paranoiac element in his makeup, and according to Freud a very close link exists between the paranoid "type" and latent homosexuality. It would not be the place here to undertake a Freudian case study of O'Hara, but it might be noted that O'Hara's pronounced interest in homosexuals and lesbians in his later period does suggest a concern that has been kept down or suppressed earlier but has finally asserted itself at the end.

2. Edward Carson, *The Fiction of John O'Hara* (Pittsburgh: University of Pittsburgh Press, 1961), p. 4.

3. Gore Vidal, "John O'Hara." In *Homage to Daniel Shays: Collected Essays 1952–1972* (New York: Random House, 1972), p. 173.

Bibliography

BOOKS BY JOHN O'HARA

Appointment in Samarra. New York: Harcourt, Brace, 1934.

The Doctor's Son and Other Stories. (Stories) New York: Harcourt, Brace, 1934.

Butterfield 8. New York: Harcourt, Brace, 1935.

Hope of Heaven. New York: Harcourt, Brace, 1938.

Files on Parade. (Stories) New York: Harcourt, Brace, 1939.

Pal Joey. (Stories) New York: Duell, Sloan & Pearce, 1940.

Pipe Night. (Stories) New York: Duell, Sloan & Pearce, 1945.

Hellbox. (Stories) New York: Random House, 1947.

A Rage to Live. New York: Random House, 1949.

The Farmers Hotel. New York: Random House, 1951.

Pal Joey: Libretto and Lyrics. New York: Random House, 1952.

Sweet and Sour. (Columns) New York: Random House, 1954.

Ten North Frederick. New York: Random House, 1955.

A Family Party. New York: Random House, 1956.

From the Terrace. New York: Random House, 1958.

Ourselves to Know. New York: Random House, 1960.

Sermons and Soda-Water. (Three novellas: *The Girl on the Baggage Truck, Imagine Kissing Pete, We're Friends Again*) New York: Random House, 1960.

Five Plays. (*The Farmers Hotel, The Searching Sun, The Champagne Pool, Veronique, The Way It Was*) New York: Random House, 1961.

Assembly. (Stories) New York: Random House, 1961.

The Big Laugh. New York: Random House, 1962.

The Cape Cod Lighter. (Stories) New York: Random House, 1962.

Elizabeth Appleton. New York: Random House, 1963.

The Hat on the Bed. (Stories) New York: Random House, 1963.

The Horse Knows the Way. (Stories) New York: Random House, 1964.

The Lockwood Concern. New York: Random House, 1965.

My Turn. (Columns) New York: Random House, 1966.

Waiting for Winter. (Stories) New York: Random House, 1966.

The Instrument. New York: Random House, 1967.

And Other Stories. (Stories) New York: Random House, 1968.

Lovey Childs: A Philadelphian's Story. New York: Random House, 1969.

Posthumous Publication

The Ewings. New York: Random House, 1972.

The Time Element and Other Stories. (Stories) New York: Random House, 1972.

Good Samaritan and Other Stories. (Stories) New York: Random House, 1974.

"An Artist Is His Own Fault": John O'Hara on Writers and Writing. Edited by Matthew J. Bruccoli. (Literary articles, speeches, and reviews) Carbondale: Southern Illinois University Press, 1977.

Selected Letters of John O'Hara. Edited by Matthew J. Bruccoli. New York: Random House, 1978.

Two by O'Hara. (*The Man Who Could Not Lose,* a screenplay, and *Far from Heaven,* a play) New York: Harcourt Brace Jovanovich, 1979.

Collections

Here's O'Hara. (*Hope of Heaven, Butterfield 8, Pal Joey,* and twenty stories) Duell, Sloan & Pearce, 1946.

All the Girls He Wanted. (Thirty-two stories) New York: Avon, 1948.

The Great Short Stories of John O'Hara. (Seventy stories) New York: Bantam, 1956.

Selected Short Stories of John O'Hara. (Thirty-two stories, with an introduction by Lionel Trilling) New York: Modern Library, 1956.

49 Stories. (*Assembly* and *The Cape Cod Lighter*, with an introduction by John K. Hutchens) New York: Modern Library, 1963.

Appointment in Samarra; Butterfield 8; Hope of Heaven. New York: Random House, 1968.

The O'Hara Generation. (Twenty-two stories, with an introduction by Albert Erskine) New York: Random House, 1969.

BOOKS ABOUT JOHN O'HARA

Bruccoli, Matthew J. *John O'Hara: A Checklist.* New York: Random House, 1972.

————. *The O'Hara Concern: A Biography of John O'Hara.* New York: Random House, 1975.

————. *John O'Hara: A Descriptive Bibliography.* Pittsburgh: University of Pittsburgh Press, 1961.

Carson, Edward, *The Fiction of John O'Hara.* (Pamphlet) Pittsburgh: University of Pittsburgh Press, 1961.

Farr, Finis. *O'Hara: A Biography.* Boston: Little, Brown, 1973.

Grebstein, Sheldon Norman. *John O'Hara.* New York: Twayne, 1966.

MacShane, Frank. *The Life of John O'Hara.* New York: Dutton, 1980.

Walcutt, Charles Child. *John O'Hara.* (Pamphlet) Minneapolis: University of Minnesota Press, 1969.

OTHER CRITICAL WRITINGS

Auchincloss, Louis, "The Novel of Manners Today: Marquand and O'Hara." In *Reflections of a Jacobite,* pp. 139–56. Boston: Houghton, Mifflin, 1961.

Bassett, Charles W. "Naturalism Revisited: The Case of John O'Hara." *Colby Library Quarterly* 11 (1975): 198–218.

Bier, Jesse. "O'Hara's *Appointment in Samarra:* His First and Only Novel." *College English* 25 (November 1963): 135–41.

Bishop, John Peale. "The Missing All." *Virginia Quarterly Review* 13 (February 1937): 106–21.

Donaldson, Scott. "Appointment with the Dentist: O'Hara's Naturalistic Novel." *Modern Fiction Studies* 14 (1968): 435–42.

Gill, Brendan. *Here at the New Yorker,* pp. 264–80. New York: Random House, 1975.

Kazin, Alfred. *On Native Grounds,* pp. 388–93. New York: Reynal & Hitchcock, 1943. Reprinted Garden City, NY: Doubleday Anchor, 1956, pp. 302–4.

———. "The Great American Bore." In *Contemporaries,* pp. 161–68. Boston: Little, Brown, 1962.

———. *Bright Book of Life,* pp. 104–110. Boston: Little, Brown, 1973.

Millgate, Michael. *American Social Fiction: James to Cozzens,* pp. 185–86.

Mizener, Arthur. Afterword. *Appointment in Samarra,* pp. 207–15. New York: New American Library Signet, 1963.

Podhoretz, Norman. "Gibbsville and New Leeds: the America of John O'Hara and Mary McCarthy." In *Doings and Undoings,* pp. 76–87. New York: Farrar, Straus & Giroux, 1964.

Portz, John. "John O'Hara Up to Now." *College English* 17 (May 1955): 493–99, 516.

Schwartz, Delmore. "Smile and Grin, Relax and Collapse." *Partisan Review* 17 (March 1950): 292–96.

See, Carolyn. "The Hollywood Novel." In *Tough Guy Writers of the Thirties,* edited by David Madden, pp. 199–217. Carbondale: Southern Illinois University Press, 1968.

Trilling, Lionel. Introduction. *Selected Short Stories of John O'Hara.* New York: Random House, 1956.

Tuttleton, James W. "John O'Hara." In *The Novel of Manners in America,* pp. 184–206. Chapel Hill: University of North Carolina Press, 1972.

Vidal, Gore. "John O'Hara." In *Homage to Daniel Shays: Collected Essays 1952–1972,* pp. 164–73. New York: Random House, 1972.

Wells, Walter. *Tycoons and Locusts: A Regional Look at Hollywood Fiction of the 1930s*, pp. 36–48. Carbondale: Southern Illinois University Press, 1973.

Wilson, Edmund. "The Boys in the Back Room." In *Classics and Commercials*, pp. 19–56. New York: Farrar, Straus & Giroux, 1950.

Index

Complete list of titles in the series available from publisher on request.